ABSTRACT ART

Author: Victoria Charles

Layout:
Baseline Co. Ltd,
District 10, Ho Chi Minh City
Vietnam

ISBN: 978-1-68325-912-1

Printed in

Victoria Charles

ABSTRACT ART

Exploring Color, Form, and Emotion in Modern Creative Expression

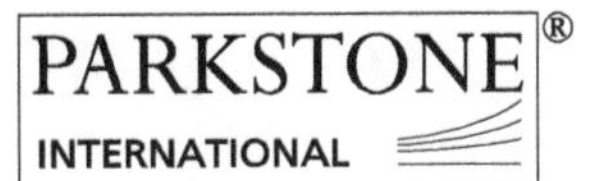

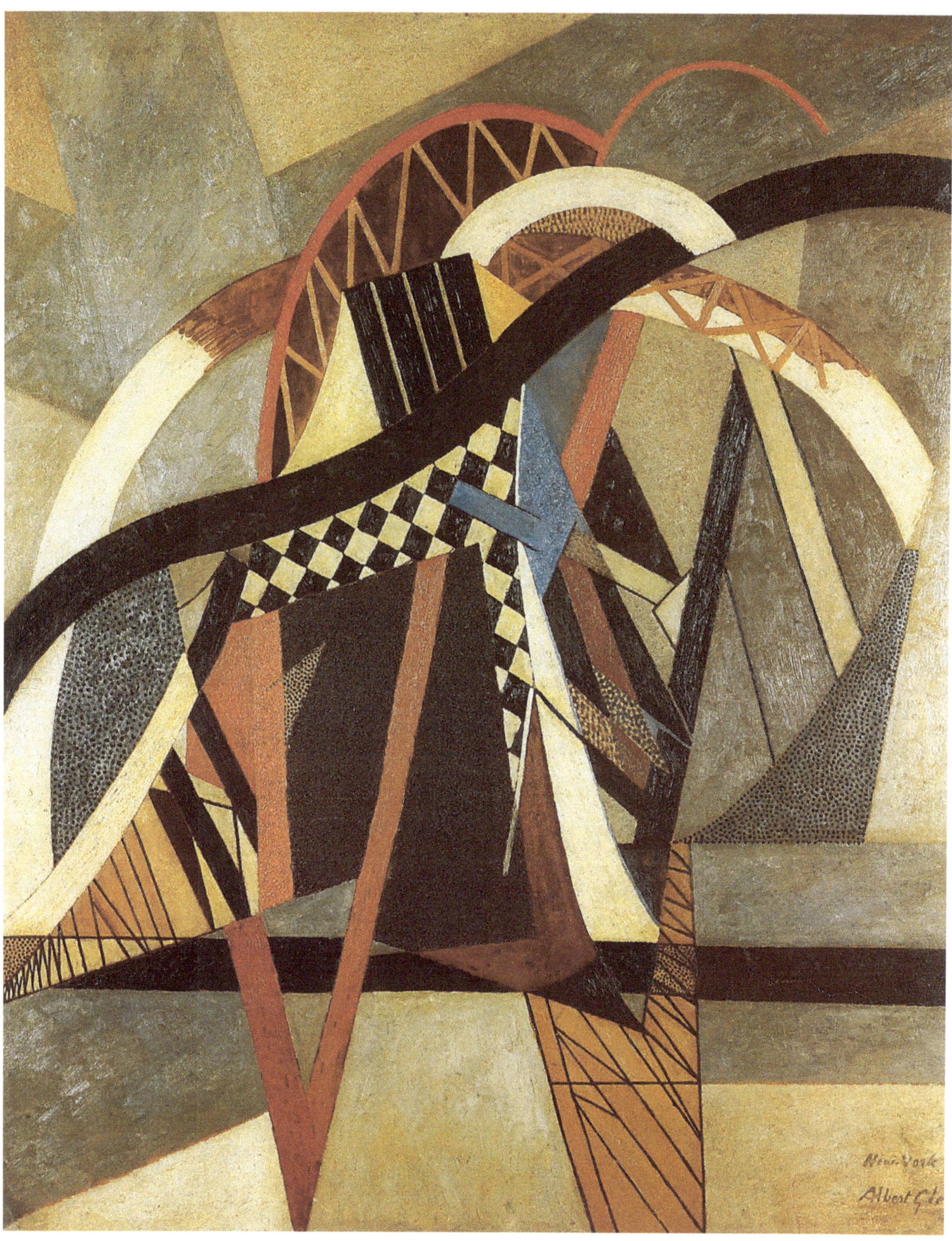

New York
Albert Gle

CONTENTS

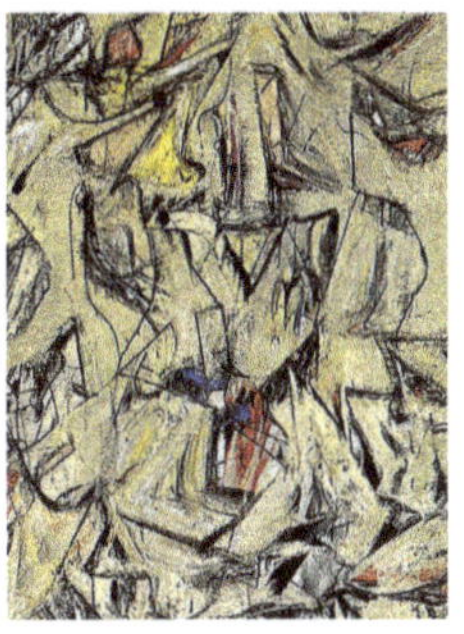

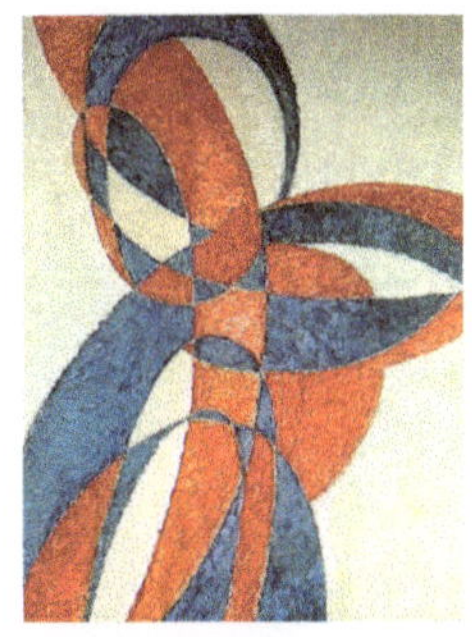

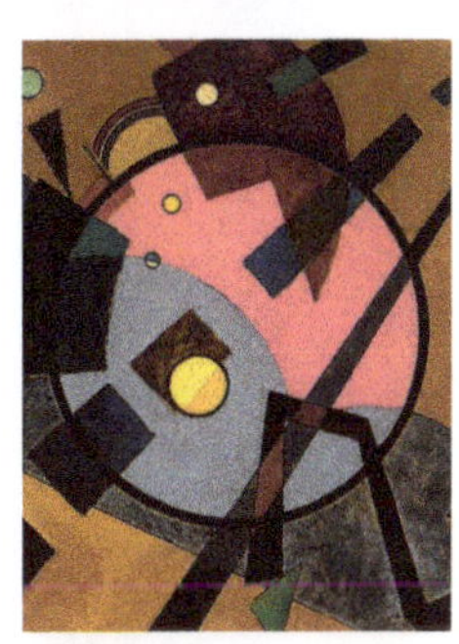

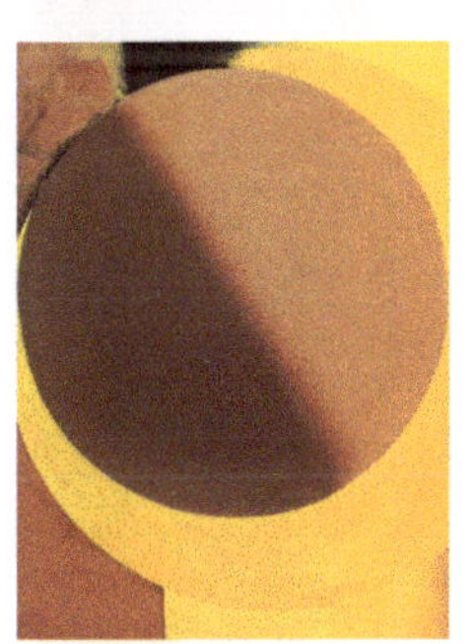

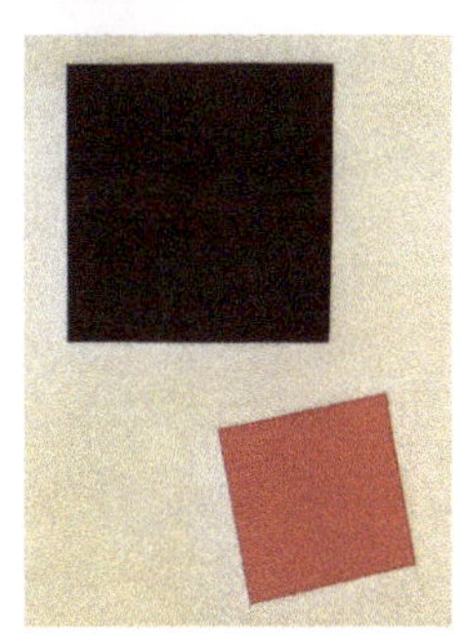

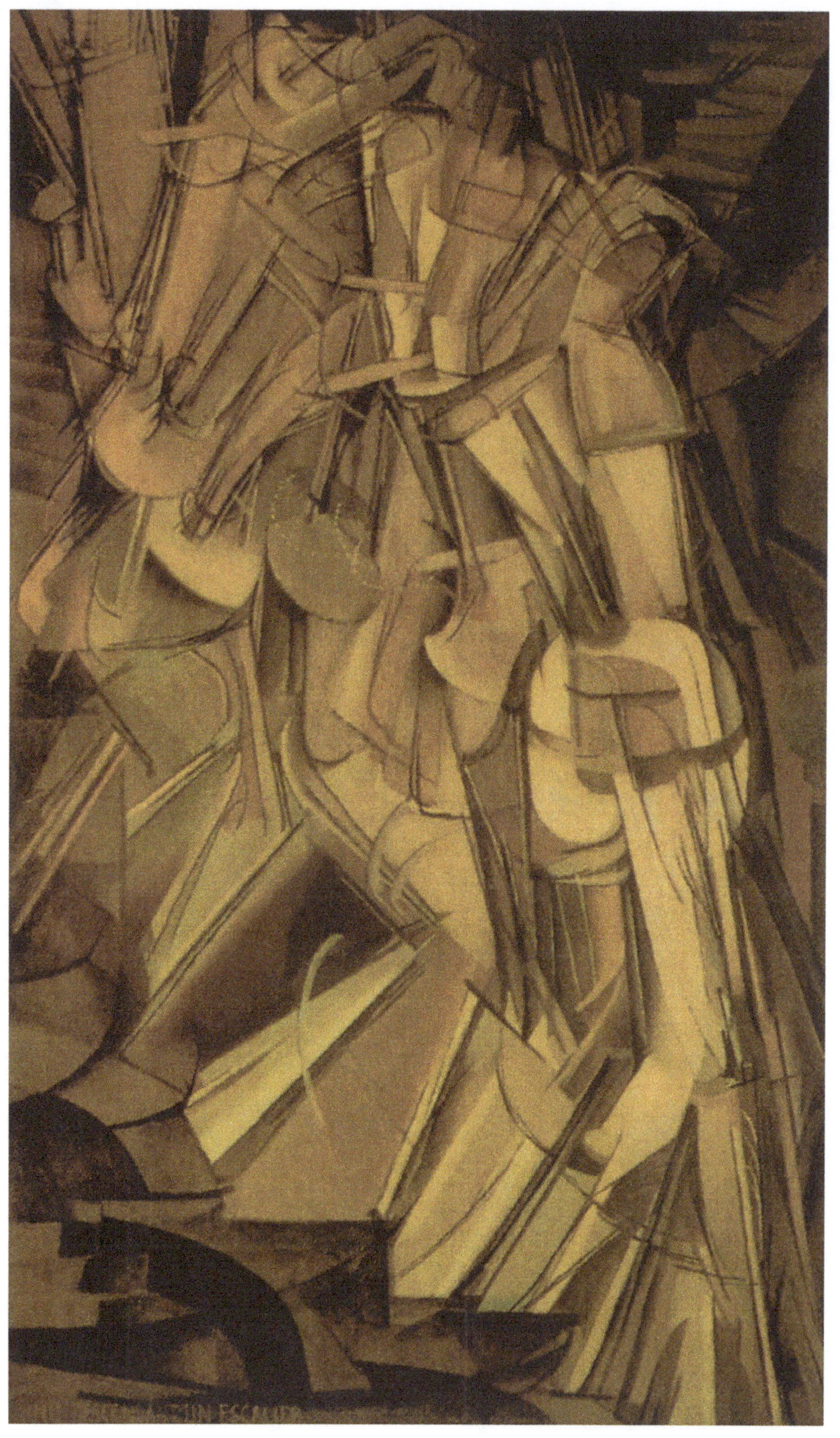

THE ORIGINS OF ABSTRACT ART

With this, the boundaries and the possibilities of artistic expression were explored to the outer limits. The divergent kaleidoscope of languages in the visual arts developed with the resulting extreme confrontations; but the overarching, all-encompassing style, which had crystallised in other centuries, was still missing. A variety of turbulent political developments, economic and social changes, technical advancement, and scientific discoveries, the wars and political tensions, as well as the rapidly advancing industrialisation had, at the close of the 19th century, led to a significant change in he existing view of the world, and to an increasing degree, a transformation of the prevailing ethical constructs. The discoveries in the natural sciences, primarily in chemistry, physics, and medicine had a huge impact on practically every person by providing a higher quality of life.

Albert Gleizes, *Brooklyn Bridge*, 1915.
Oil on cardboard, 148.1 x 120.4 cm.
Private collection.

Marcel Duchamp, *Nude descending a Staircase*, No. 2, 1912.
Oil on canvas, 147.5 x 89.2 cm.
Louise and Walter Arensberg collection, Philadelphia
Museum of Art, Philadelphia.

Visual habits changed with the introduction of the car, radio, and telephone because of the new speeds and the manner of seeing things from great heights, from aircraft, hot air balloons, and from tall buildings.

Scientific research, and the discoveries which resulted, radically altered the way people conceptualised the world around them. In 1895, Wilhelm Conrad Röntgen discovered Röntgen rays, better known as X-rays, and suddenly, it was possible to see inside of a person. In 1900, Max Planck developed with quantum theory, which contradicted the very basis of traditional physics. In the same year, the world was shaken by the psychoanalytic interpretations of Sigmund Freud, giving further insight into a person's innermost feelings and motivations. Shortly thereafter, Hermann Minkowski developed the mathematical model to describe the space-time dimension, which in turn led his student, Albert Einstein, to develop his famous theory of general relativity.

Since around 1890, fundamental changes have occurred in the art of Western cultures. These developments were born from the desire for pure, unconditional vision. Over the years, it was no longer visual improvement of an object that was the goal of artistic expression, but rather the depiction of the 'second reality'. Therefore, that became the goal of artistic creation.

At the beginning of the 20th century, trends started to emerge that began to diverge from a naturalistic conception of reality and set out to explore beneath the mere superficial appearance of things. Regardless of the multitude of stylistic backgrounds in individual Western countries, everywhere, the new realisation that a work of art ought no longer to be made in the spirit of the old aesthetics of imitation, as if taken from nature, but rather rise from its own independent dimension of existence. A work of art is now autonomous.

The inner mission of the artist was no longer to portray or interpret, as in the previous centuries, for photography had perfected that aim. Invented and developed by two Frenchmen, Jacques Mandé Daguerre and Joseph Nicéphore Niépce, between 1822 and 1838, photography increasingly competed with painting as a means to document events and to depict situations. However, it was also helpful to artists as an aid to a broadened vision.

Almost all modernist artistic movements received their momentum from the new visual relationship to the non-stationary object that had suddenly revealed itself to be a mobile and fragmented. Despite the artistic developments of individual countries, all innovative artists were united in the common search for a new graphic style of movement, one which encompassed a sense of autonomous colour creation and an abstract language of independent forms. In 1905, the Fauves, the new wild ones, displayed their subversive explosions of colour at the Salon d'Automne in Paris.

Expressionism started in Germany in 1905 with the founding of the Dresden artist group, Die Brücke. In 1907, Paris dedicated an extensive exhibition to the works of Paul Cézanne. It was at this exhibit that Georges Braque and Pablo Picasso came into contact with the gray shades of Cubism, which rejected the perspective of the Renaissance, fragmented the visual world, and radically separated the world of painting from that of natural phenomenon. The Cubists stemmed from Cezanne with tremendous reinforcements from Picasso, Braque, Leger, Gris. They strove for the geometric constants of form, decomposed natural objects into their form elements, and with these tried to create new objects capable of stirring us by their art qualities alone. It was immaterial to Cubists whether these retained or lost all semblances to natural objects. Marcoussis, Lurcat, Delaunay and Picabia contributed their influence.

In 1911, the Cubists exhibited for the first time at the Paris Salon d'Automne. The same year in Paris, Robert Delaunay developed Orphism, which sought to give colours their autonomy. In Italy, Emilio Filippo Tommaso Marinetti founded Futurism, a vocal movement that infused the visual world with a net of dynamic energy. His first manifesto was published in February 1909 in Paris. The Futurist

Juan Gris,
Still Life (Violin and Ink Pot), 1913.
Oil on canvas, 89.5 x 60.5 cm.
Kunstsammlung Nordrhein-Westfalen, Düsseldorf.

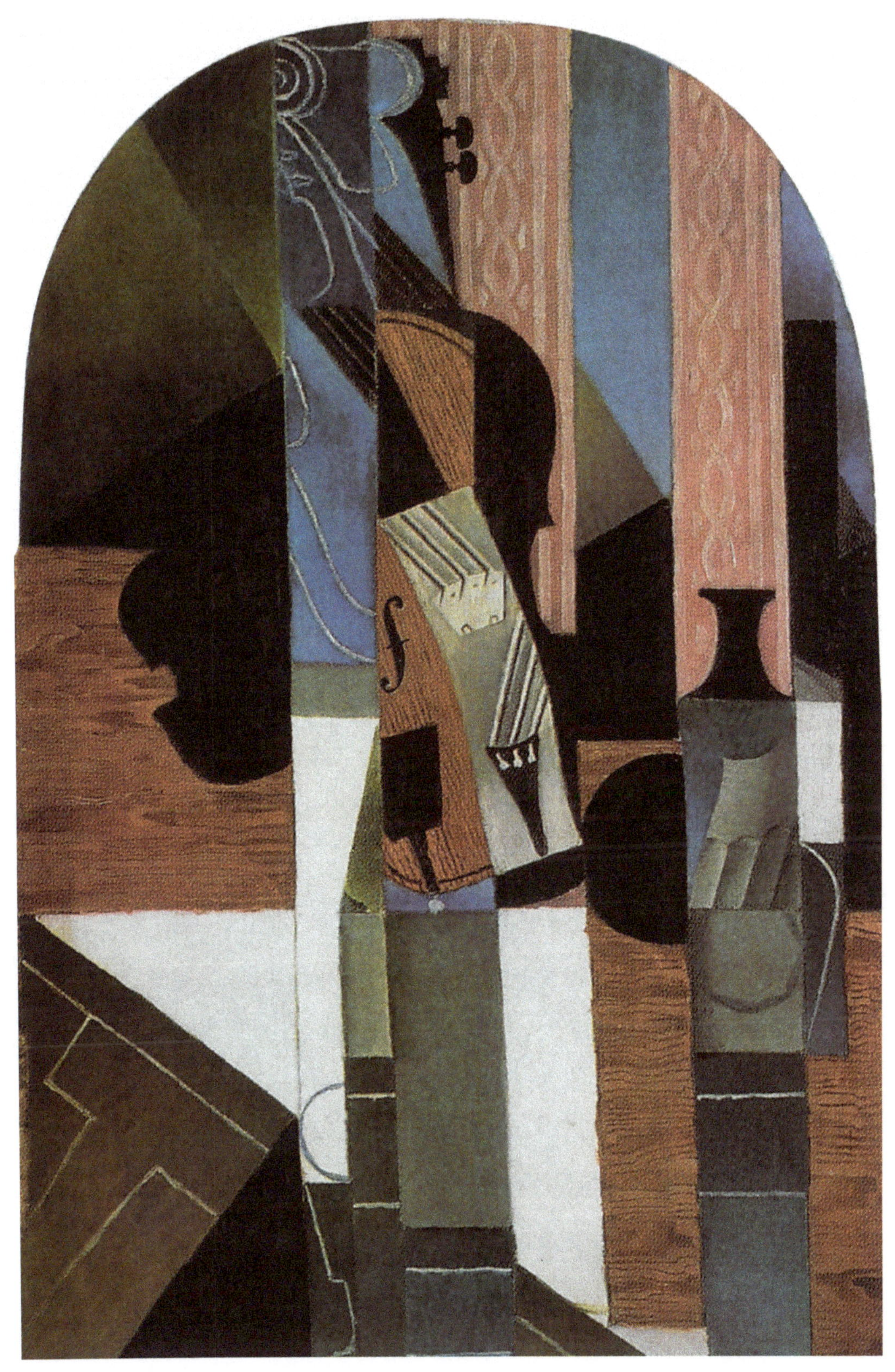

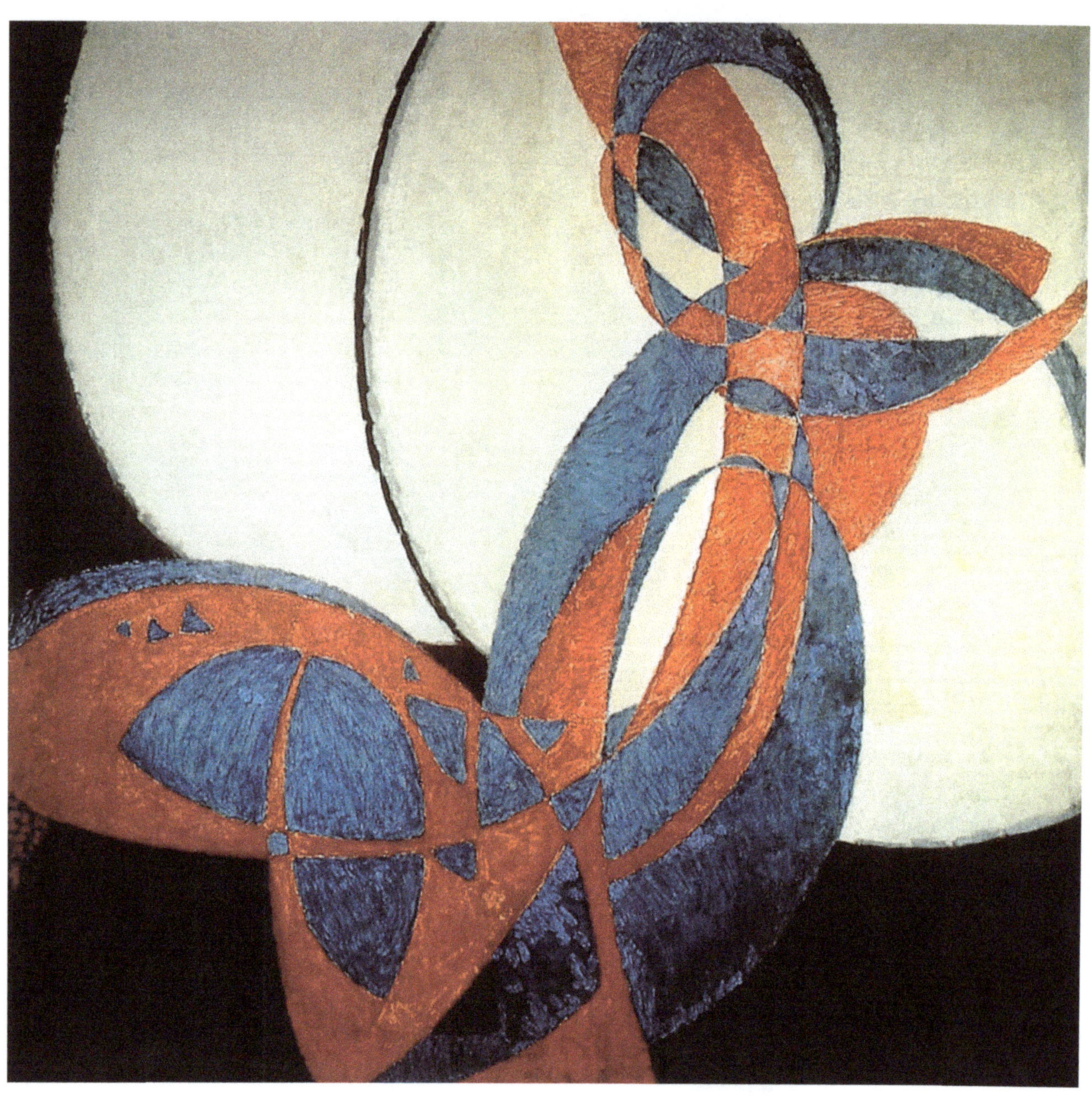

painters announced their first manifestos in 1910. In 1909, the Neue Künstlervereinigung (New Artists' Association) was formed in Munich. Der Blaue Reiter (The Blue Rider) would later emerge from this around the intellectual centre of Kandinsky and Marianne von Werefkin. In early 1912, a touring exhibit of Futurist painters began in Paris that would trigger a veritable avalanche of explosive painting genres in almost all Western-oriented countries.

Around 1910, purely nonrepresentational art was introduced independently — but virtually simultaneously — by artists in several countries. Wassily Kandinsky in Germany, Frantisek Kupka in France, Piet Mondrian in the Netherlands, Kazimir Malevich in Russia, and Arthur Dove in the United States were among the most influential of these artists. Its beginnings were formulated by Kandinsky's vision of an 'era of the great spiritual.' One finds origins of concrete art with Kupka, Mondrian, and Malevich, as well as with Georges Vantongerloo. The term 'Concrete Art' was coined by Theo van Doesburg in his Manifesto of Concrete Art of 1930. He suggested the term 'concrete' for an art based solely on pure relationships of form and colour.

Despite their concentration on the arrangement of non referential form and colour, many of these artists professed that philosophical and spiritual considerations inspired their artistic endeavours. Hardly any other art movement during the 20th century changed our perception and our visible world as much as abstract art (also called concrete, nonrepresentational, constructive, or nonfigurative).

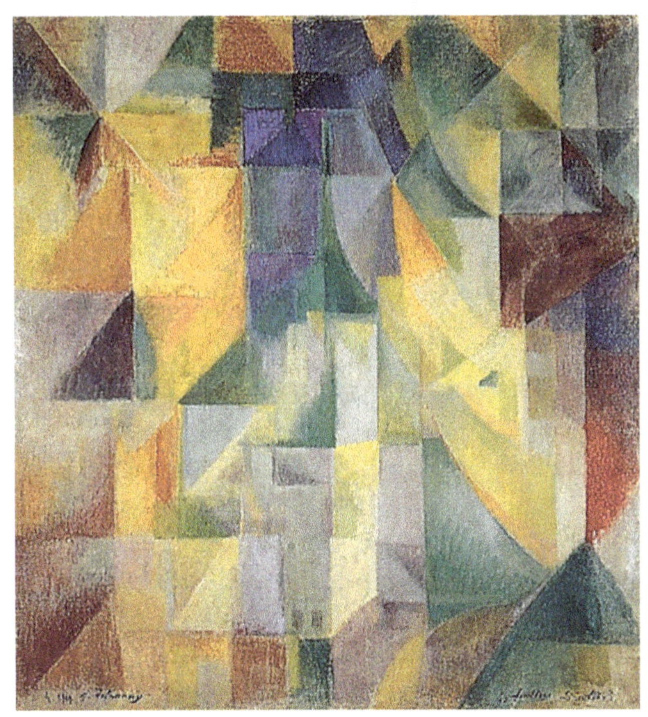

František Kupka, *Apathetic — Escape in Two Colours*, 1912.
Oil on canvas, 211 x 220 cm.
Národní Gallery, Prague.

Robert Delaunay, *Windows*, 1912.
Oil on canvas, 92 x 86 cm.
Morton G. Neumann collection, Chicago.

Wassily Kandinsky, *Composition VII*, 1913.
Oil on canvas, 200 x 300 cm.
Tretyakov State Gallery, Moscow.

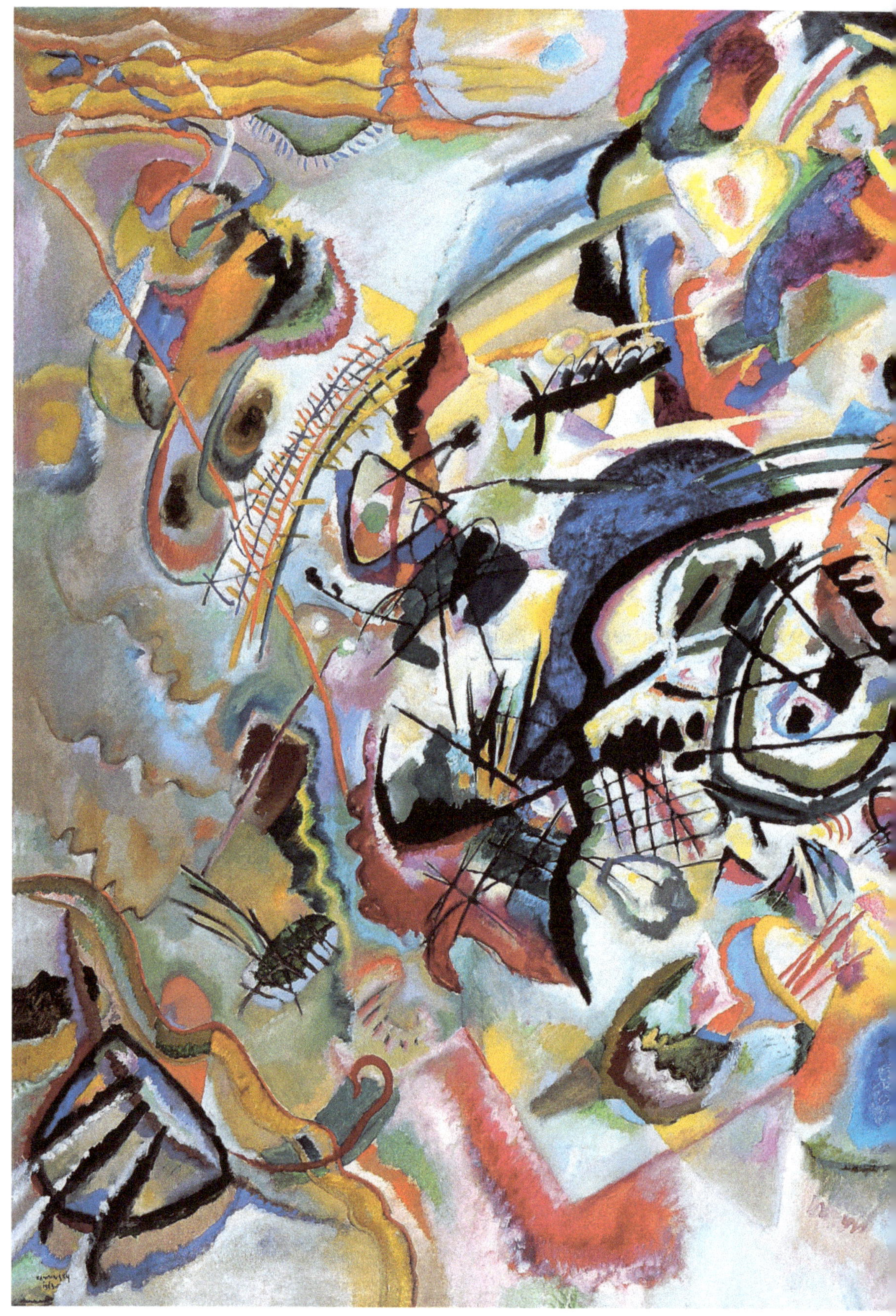

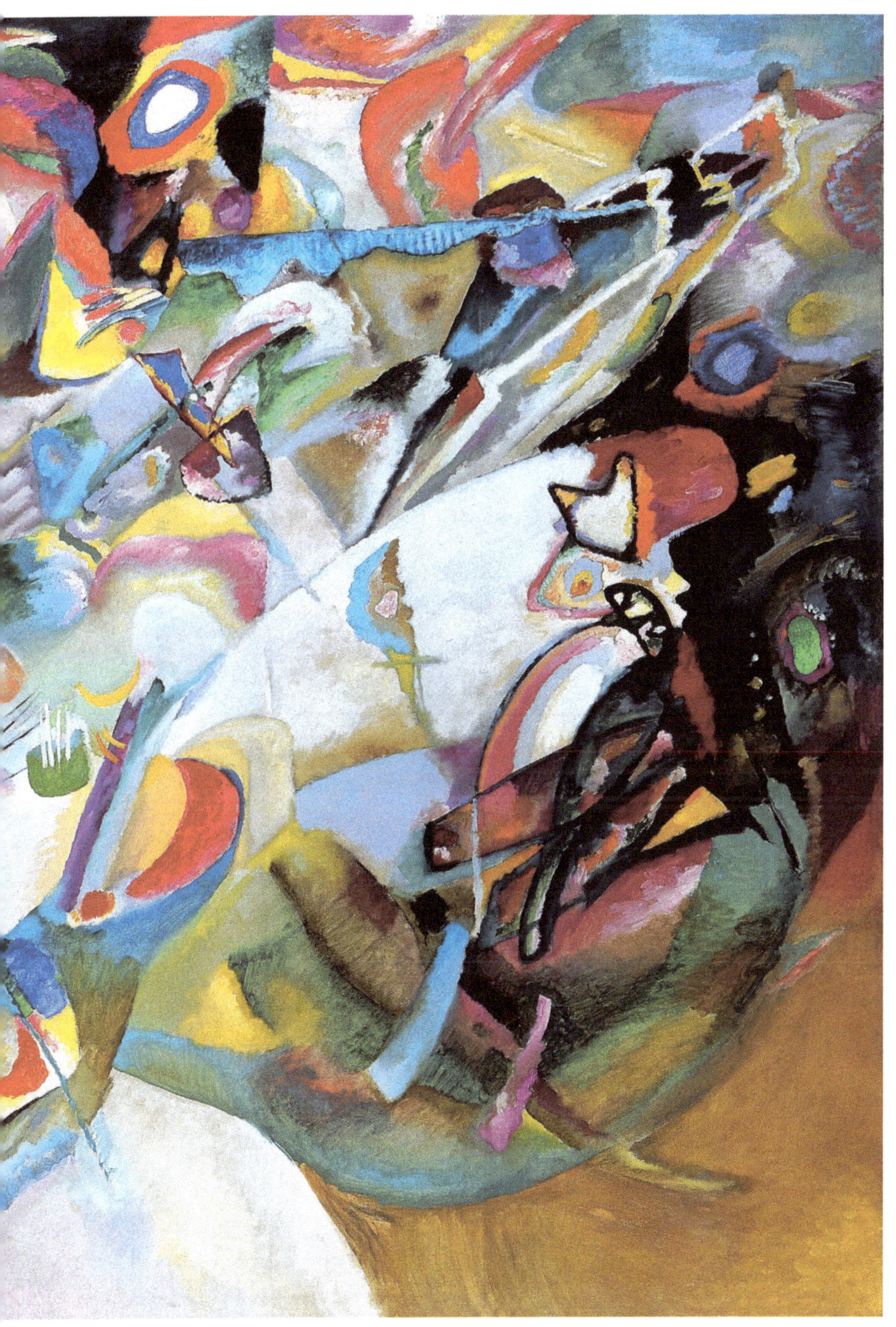

THE RUSSIAN AVANT-GARDE - EXCHANGE BETWEEN EAST AND WEST

The Russian avant-garde is one of the most surprising intellectual and creative movements in the art of the 20th century. Within a very short time, an immensely concentrated burst of the most varied creative innovations emanated from Moscow and Leningrad. In the 18th century, Russia had opened itself up to the West, primarily to France and Germany and the lively exchange in the intellectual and artistic spheres between the East and West during the first two decades of the 20th century unleashed an innovative and mutually enriching art scene of the highest calibre. The new discoveries in the spheres of physics, technology, medicine, and psychology, were the basis of this scientific-artistic questioning. The eastern and western avant-gardes were a closely woven conglomerate of reciprocal inspiration. One cannot imagine the non-representational art of the west without the trail blazing of a Frantisek, Kupka, or Wassily Kandinsky. De Stijl cannot be imagined without Suprematism and eastern Constructivism. Many of the *émigrés*, who were successful in the west, had their roots in the east like the Romanian Constantin Brancusi, or the Russian Marc Chagall.

The Russians were primarily drawn to France and Germany. Wassily Kandinsky, like Alexej von Jawlensky, and Marianne von Werefkin, had already had travelled to Munich in 1896 and often returned to Russia. Léon Bakst, Marc Chagall, Antoine Pevsner, and El Lissitzky lived and worked in the years 1910 and 1914 in either France or Germany. Archipenko and Survage went to Paris in 1908, as did Zadkine and Lipchitz a year later. After the outbreak of World War I in 1914, they brought their experience back to their Russian homeland. Mikhail Larionov and Natalia Gontcharova went in the opposite direction and immigrated to Paris in 1917.

From around 1905 until the 1920s, Russian art, driven by creative and intellectual energy, developed in an unusually multifaceted manner. Neo-Primitivism, Cubo-Futurism and Abstract Expressionism, Rayonism, Suprematism and Constructivism followed this all the way to Analytic Art. With respect to painting, the most

Kazimir Malevich, *Black Square on White Background*, dated of 1913, achieved after 1920.
Oil on canvas, 106.2 x 106.5 cm.
Russian Museum, St. Petersburg.

outstanding representatives of this multifaceted, yet very intense, period are Natalia Gontcharova, Wassily Kandinsky, Mikhail Larionov, Kazimir Malevich, Mikhail Matyuchin, and El Lissitzky.

The Russian Avant-Garde of the 1920s-1930s gave birth to several major schools of art whose disciples founded their work on the unique principles defined by their leaders, in particular, Malevich and Matiushin. The work of Kuzma Petrov-Vodkin and his followers constitutes one of the summits of Soviet art in the 1920s-1930s. In his thesis about transcending visual attraction and gravity, Malevich managed to express the great principle of the new 'comprehension of space' that unites them all. Larionov's Rayonism, Kandinsky's Abstract Art, Malevich's Suprematism and Filonov's Analytical Method were, despite all their differences, systems based on the principle of transcending attraction. The structures that appeared in their work were referring to a world more universal than the one in which attraction reigns.

Shchukin had already opened his collection of contemporary art to the public in Moscow in 1914. What significance this collection of the French avant-garde had for the specific development of Russian art before the revolutions can be judged by what the painter, David Burliuk, one of the future Cubo-Futurists, said, as he wrote to a friend in St Petersburg: "In Moscow, we often looked at the French collections of both S. I. Shchukin and I. A. Morozov. If I had not, I would not have dared to start. We have been at home now for three days. All the old stuff has been thrown into the rubbish heap, and, oh, it is hard and uplifting to start again from the beginning".

A unique ensemble of paintings by Paul Gauguin, placed close together like a frieze in the manner of an Old Russian iconostasis, was on display in the Shchukin's dining room. Located in the centre was the painting *Obsterte* (*Fruit Harvest*) from the last Tahiti period. Natalia Gontcharova, deeply impressed, responded to Paul Gauguin with her four-piece composition *Fruit Harvest*.

She painted an equally exotic depiction of daily life, however, one with Russian folkloric motifs, lifting the simple, daily life of the Russian peasant to her *Tahiti*, into her paradise-like state. Never before had the artistic relations between Russia and France been so intense. The legendary *The Golden Fleece* exhibition of 1908, named after the journal of the same name, reflected this. On display were 282 paintings, two thirds of which were from Paris. For the first time, many Russian artists saw Cézanne, Degas, Gauguin, Van Gogh, Renoir, Pissarro and the Nabis with Bonnard, Denis, Vuillard, Sérusier, and the Pointillists. What impressed the Russians the most were the Fauves like Derain, Marquet, Matisse and van Dongen. The impact of this exhibit on the evolving Russian avant-garde cannot be overestimated.

As a result, two distinct groups arose. In St Petersburg, the *Union of Youth,* and in Moscow, *Jack of Diamonds* led by Larionov and Gontcharova. Their place was taken in 1911 by the group

Pavel Filonov,
Faces, 1940.
Oil on paper, 64 x 56 cm.
The State Russian Museum, St Petersburg.

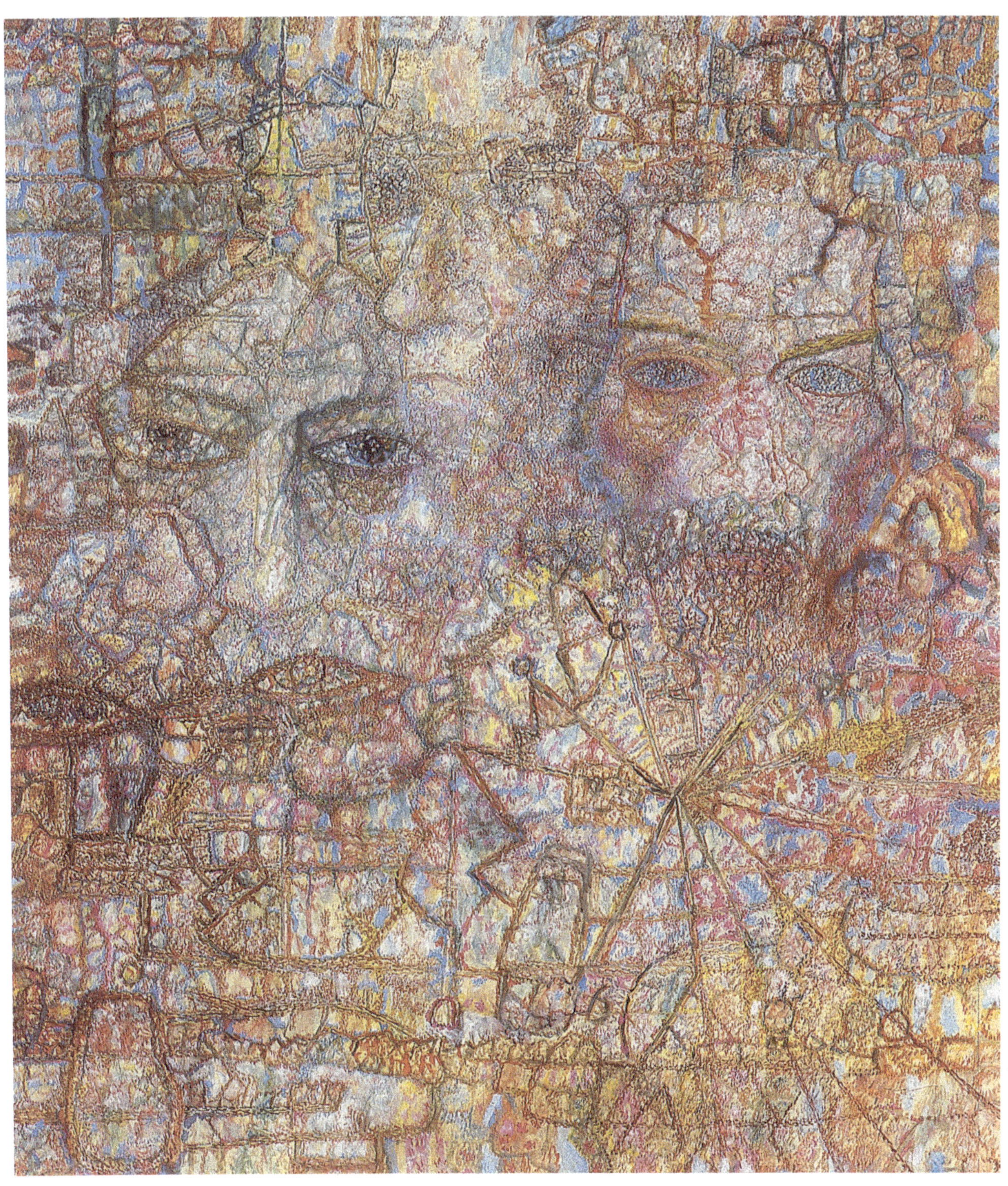

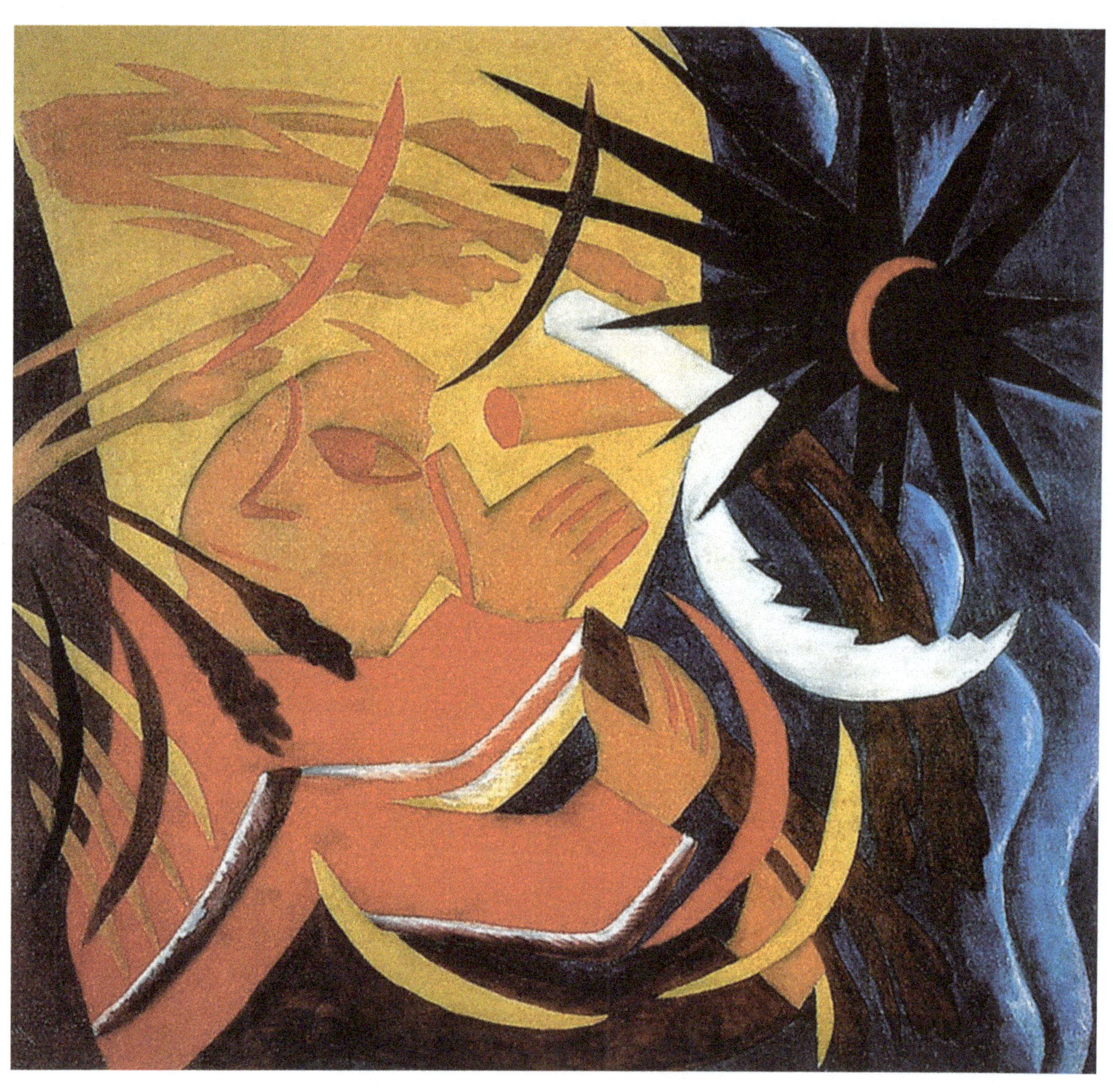

Natalia Gontcharova, *The Harvest*, 1911.
Oil on canvas, 92 x 99 cm. Musée des Beaux-Arts, Omsk.

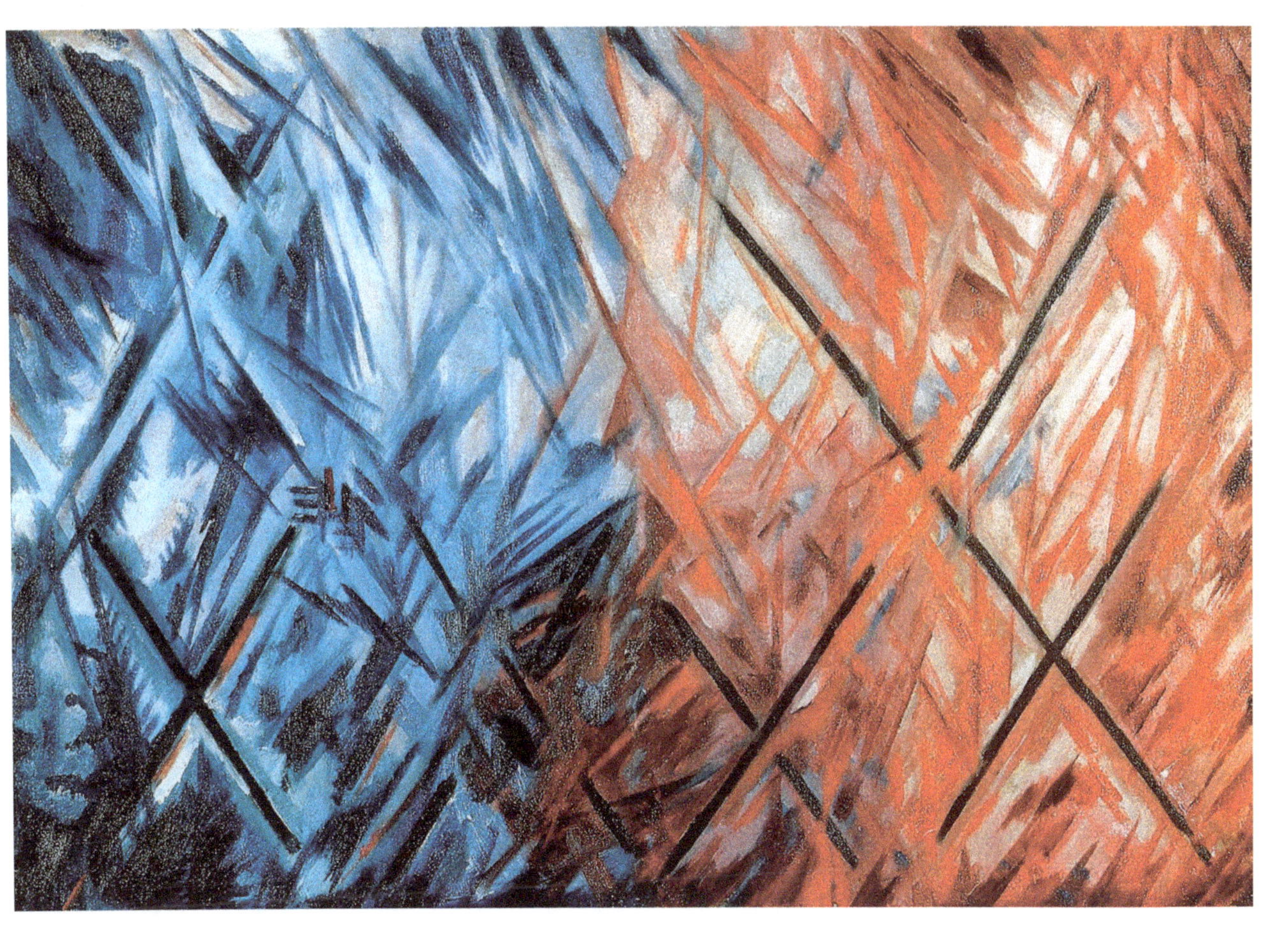

Mikhail Larionov, *Rayonism*, 1912-13.
Oil on canvas, 52.5 x 78.5 cm. Baschkirski Museum, Ufa.

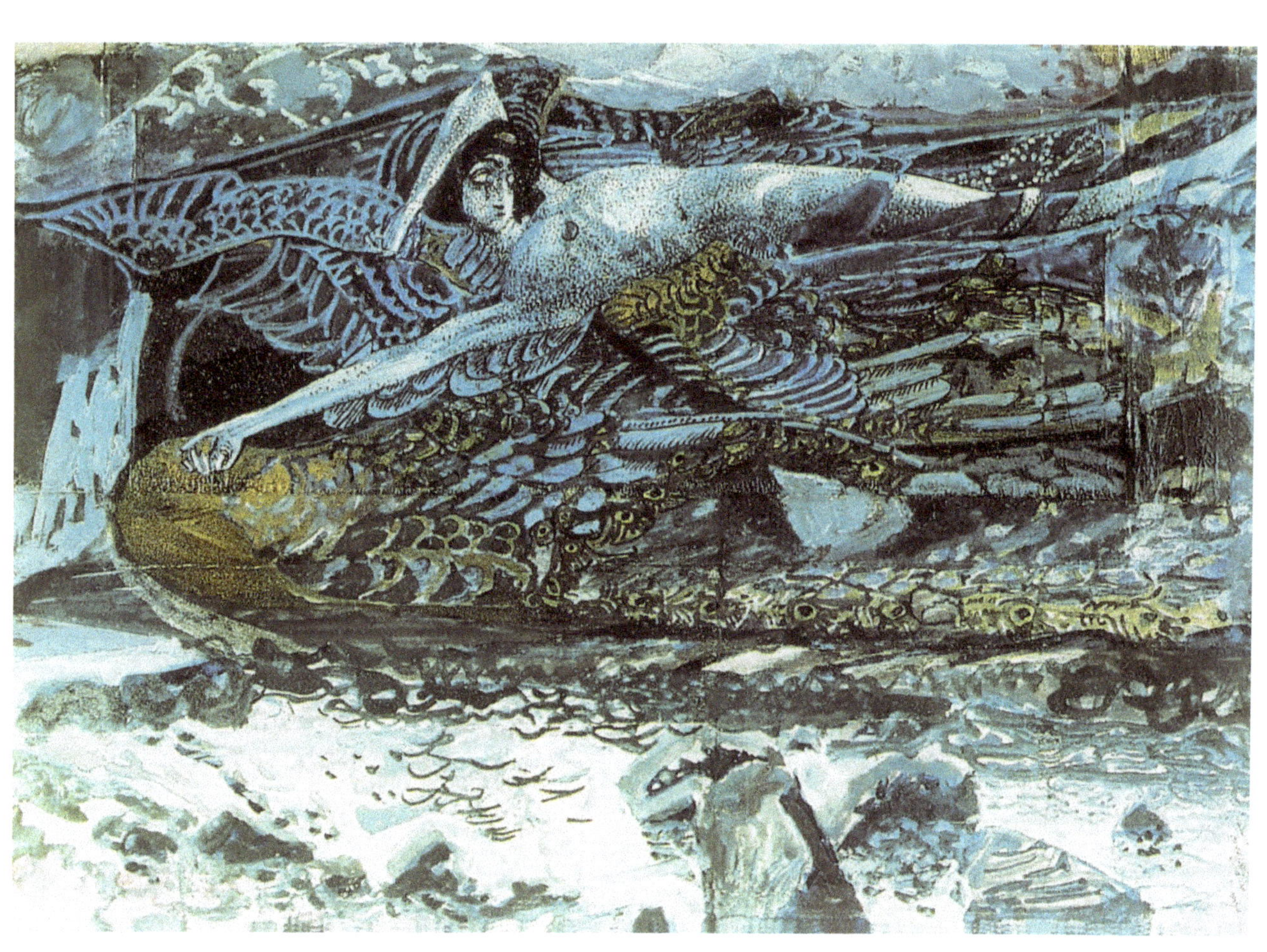

Donkey's Tail, with whom Tatlin and Malevich exhibited, and, in 1913, by the group, *Target*. For the prerevolutionary Moscow art scene, the activities of Larionov and his wife, Gontcharova, were of crucial importance. Before World War I, both took part in a number of exhibits abroad, for example, in 1912 with the Blaue Reiter in Munich and at the *Erste Deutsche Herbstsalon* in Berlin. Larionov travelled a further time in 1914 to Paris in order to work there with Diaghilev at his ballet. Together with Gontcharova, he exhibited in Paris, and wrote the foreword to the catalogue.

Italian Futurism also contributed important ideas to the Russian intellectual life. The short-lived Cubo-Futurism group, which in addition to Mikhail Larionov and Natalia Gotcharova, Aleksandra Ekster, David Burliuk, Lyubov Popova and Kazimir Malevich belonged, united Futurist ideas on painting with those of the Russian Neo-Primitivists. Out of this developed the almost object-free Rayonism style. In Saint Petersburg, the Futurists met with Matyuchin and Elena Guro. In addition, the brothers Burliuk, Vasily Kamensky, Kazimir Malevich, Vladimir Mayakovsky and Olga Rozanova also took part.

Rayonism

From 1912 to 1913, the Russian avant-garde developed a strong sense of personal identity of its own and looked increasingly to the strengths and values of its own national origins. Larionov together with Gontcharova created Rayonism, an early variant of abstract art. They, thereby, sought primarily to differentiate themselves from Italian Futurism. In the Manifesto of Rayonism, written in 1912 and published in 1913, they expressly praised nationalism.

Rayonism combined contemporary European trends. It fused Cubism and Futurism in so far as it fragmented and energised the painting surface. It fused Orphism in so far as it realised the dynamic quality of the light by means of colour contrasts. For Mikhail Larionov, Rayonism (Rayon = beam) meant the dissolution of the painting subject. He referred to the scientific research regarding the materiality of light. This he visualised in his paintings through a bundle of rays and refractions through a prism. A depiction referring to an object had hardly any meaning for him. His concern was only about depicting the phenomenon of radiating energy that attaches to all things. He treated shape and colour as autonomous elements. In the *Manifesto of Rayonism*, Larionov speaks about '... the rays of things that the artist subjects to his expressive desire. The painting appears as such not of space and time; it spews out sensations that let us sense the fourth dimension.'

The *Manifesto of Rayonism* became instructive for Suprematism to the degree as Malevich states: Long live our Rayonistic painting style, which is independent of shapes belonging to reality and develops accordingly to artistic laws. It concerns itself with spatial forms that result from the reflection of intersecting rays of various objects,

Mikhail Vrubel, *Fallen Demon*, 1901.
Watercolour, gouache on paper,
sketch for 1902's painting, 21 x 30 cm.
Drawings department, The Pushkin Museum of Fine Arts,
Moscow.

and it rests upon shapes that are determined by the artist himself. Following his trip to London in 1906, where the watercolours of William Turner had impressed him, Mikhail Larionov had become obsessed with the idea of a non-figurative painting. Now with Rayonism, he had been able to realise his vision.

Matyushin and Malevich.

The painter and musician, Mikhail Vasilyevich Matyushin, assumed among the Russian avant-garde a leading and, for the younger generation, an influential position. He was a professional musician, painter and an intellectual. In the years between 1903 and 1905 he had experimented in the area of quartertone music. In addition, he was interested in science and philosophy. In the correspondence between Kazimir Severinovich, Malevich and Matyushin, it becomes apparent that it was Matyushin, who for a considerable period of time conveyed the developments in philosophical theories such as the teachings of Berdyaev, Fyodorov, or Bergson, as well as mystical theories of the Middle Ages and ancient Indian philosophy to Malevich. Both artists were bound by a lifelong friendship. Of the two, Matyushin was closer to nature, he felt as though elements of painting should be analogous to those found in nature and beings found in the organic world.

Malevitch, *Red Square, motif: 1915*, version: c. 1916-1917.
Oil on canvas, 53 x 53 cm.
The State Russian Museum, St. Petersburg.

Matyushin undertook exercises to increase his perception in order to intuitively understand and anticipate the hidden and supernatural.

In 1913 Malevich and Matyushin jointly produced the opera *Victory over the Sun*. This became a milestone in the development of art in the 20th century. Malevich designed the costumes and the set. The poet, Kroutchenykh, wrote the libretto and Velemir Khlebnikov wrote the prologue. Matyuchin's futuristically oriented composition, which incorporated dissonances, unexpected interval jumps, aircraft noises, cannons, and machines, inspired Malevich to develop Suprematism. This opera was the first attempt at a total show, a precursor of later innovation. On the curtains between the acts, Malevich had painted his first *Black Square*.

From 1912 and 1913, Malevich's works become increasingly abstract. Cézanne's goal to geometrise everything led him more and more to abstract shapes that organise space in three dimensions. Malevich had succeeded in producing a convincing synthesis of Cubism and Futurism in these paintings. He succeeded in the fracturing and energising of the world of shapes and, furthermore, like Matisse, in the emancipation of colour.

Fernand Léger succeeded in arriving at a similar form of expression at the same time in Paris. This was just at the time when in 1912 the vehement dispute over priorities between the Cubists and the Futurists broke out. Léger and Malevich solved this problem in their own way. Indeed, they rather built their paintings, as it were, out of elements shaped

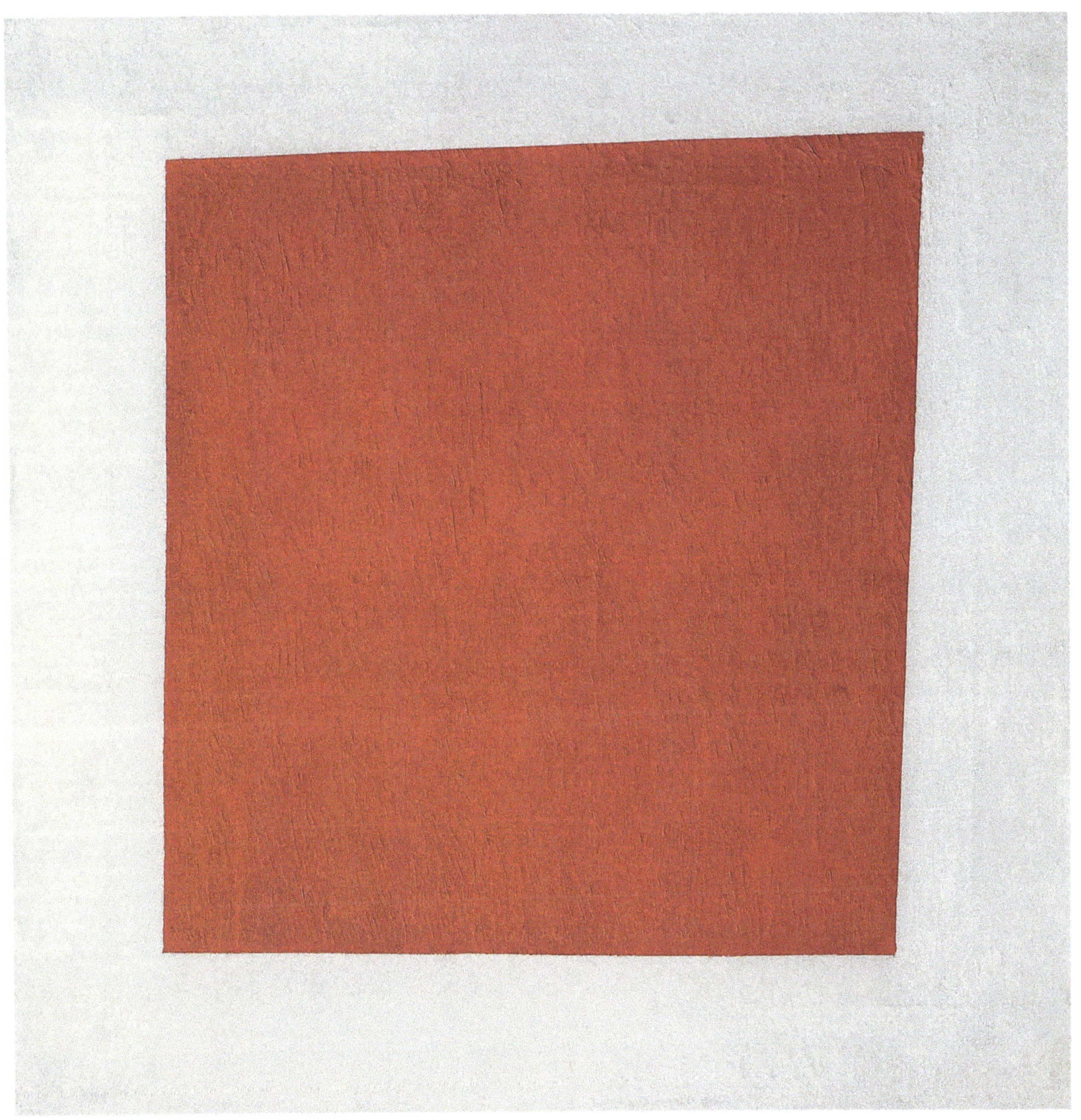

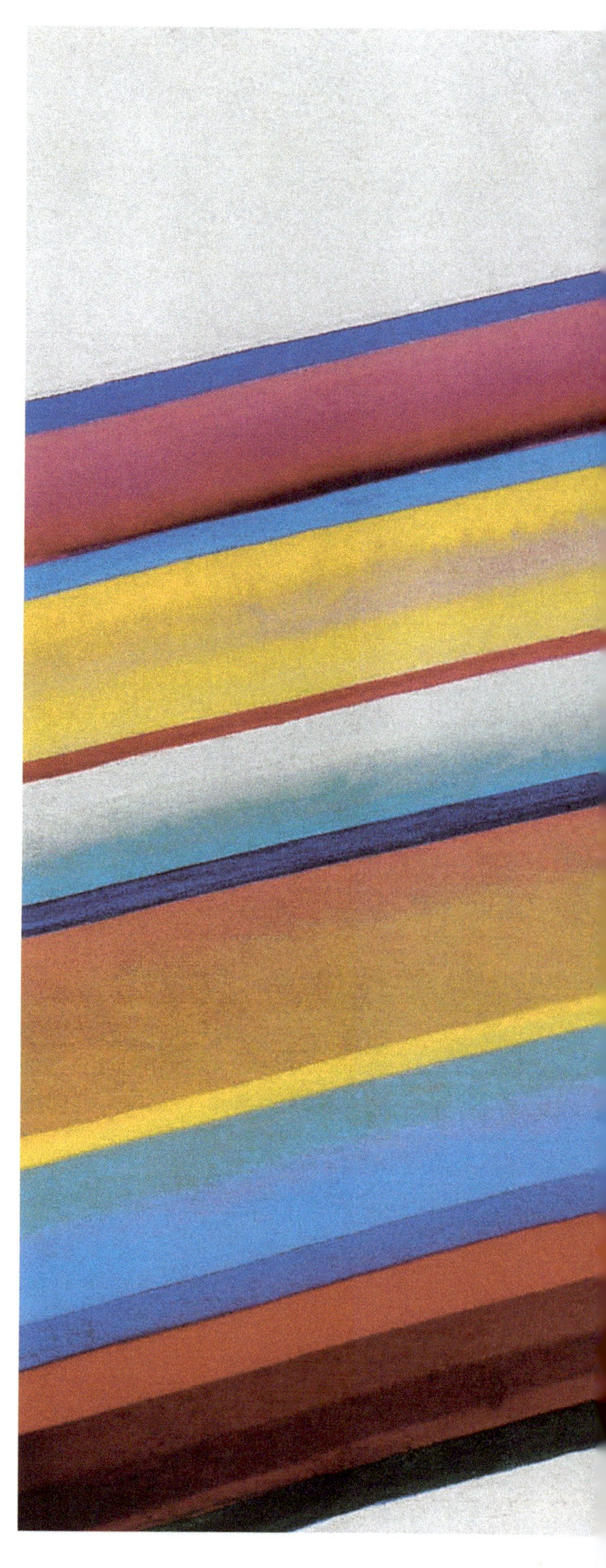

Michail Matyuchin, *Moving into Space*, 1919.
Oil on canvas, 124 x 168 cm.
Russian Museum, St. Petersburg.

24

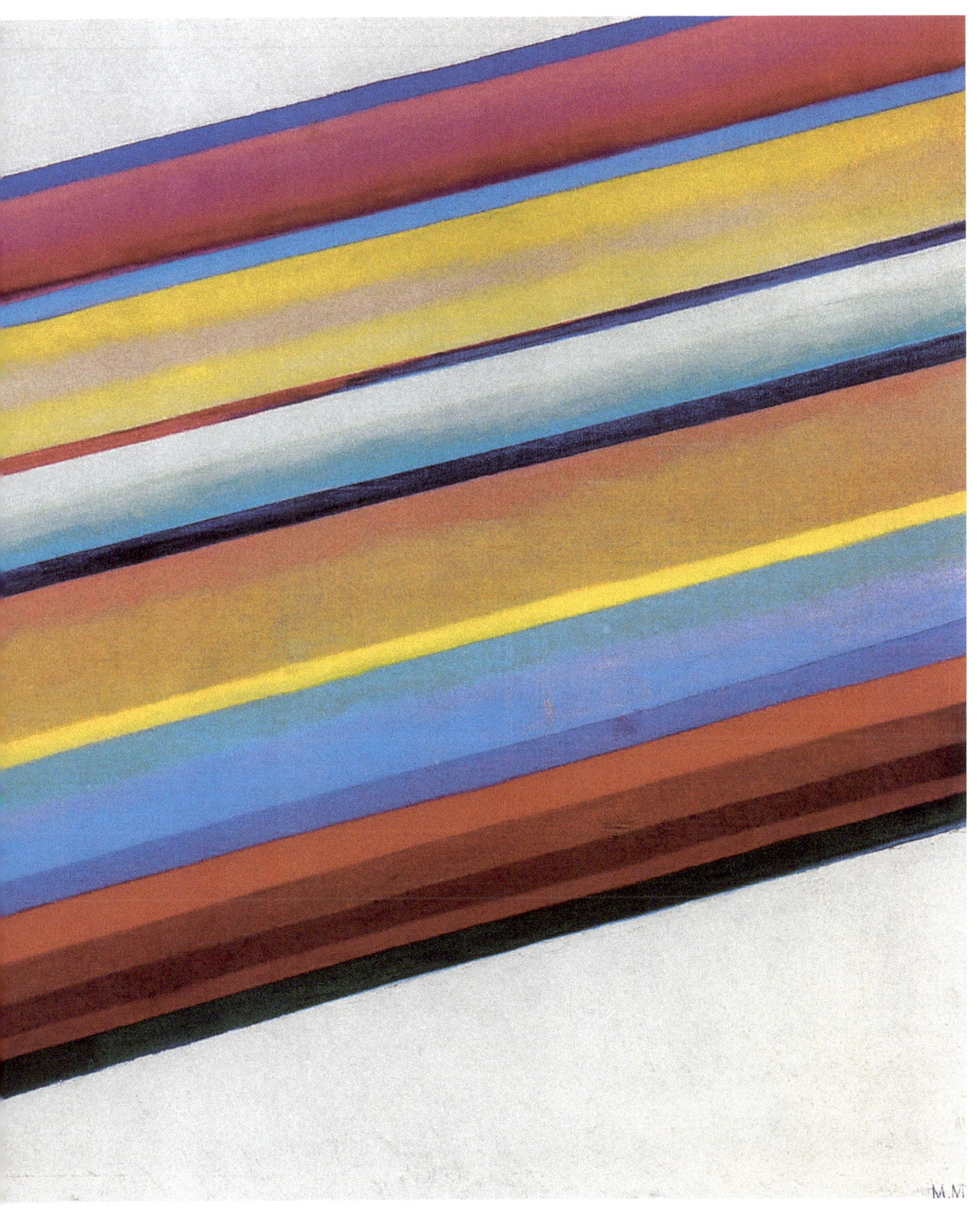

25

like pipes of such volume that they fit one in the other and in this manner create a strong dynamic effect. To the colour they mixed metallic elements, thereby, stressing the mechanical.

In subsequent years, Malevich came ever closer to the higher level of consciousness of 'pure painting.' This was certainly encouraged by the theories of Nikolai Berdyaev, who had been teaching in Moscow since 1917 and had founded a Religious Philosophical Academy. His spiritual teachings regarding the relativity and equilibrium of man and the cosmos convinced Malevich that he could create perfect supermatistic shapes that float in themselves.

Pure Painting: Suprematism

Kazimir Malevich is the leading figure of abstract art. He was a founder of Suprematism and paved the way for Constructivism (which he rejected). He derived his theories mainly from French and German Expressionism, Cubism and Futurism. At the last Futurist Zero-Ten in St Petersburg during the December of 1915, he exhibited his work *Black Square on a White Surface*.

The *Black Square on a White Surface* became the icon of modernist art, a key work of abstract art. It has no other meaning than itself. It has no meaning. It is.

Malevitch, *Painterly Realism. Boy with Knapsack – Colour Masses in the Fourth Dimension*, 1915.
Oil on canvas, 71.1 x 44.4 cm.
The Museum of Modern Art, New York.

Malevich coined the term Suprematism which means the same as 'totality without a subject' or 'new realistic painting.' Malevich published the *Manifesto of Suprematism* in 1915. In it he formulated visions that threw overboard all previous ideas about art. He ranked the perception of abstractness above that of shape. A square, a circle, a triangle or a cross on a neutral surface is 'by its nature no longer an imposing painting.' His geometric elements were restricted to the greatest simplicity and permitted no relation to reality. He, thereby, had already formulated important concepts at the turn of the century that would become fundamental for the concept art of the 1970s, American Minimalist art and many contemporary artists. The brothers Antoine Pevsner and Naum Gabo also spoke out in favour of a new sculpture of the 'abstract' in their 1920 manifesto, which they named *Realistic Manifesto.*

After the 1917 October Revolution, Malevich taught at the State Art School in Moscow. From 1919 onwards he took part in the creation of the modern teaching institute in Vitebsk. However, in 1921 the official attacks on his art began. Malevich was dismissed from all his official duties; however, he was allowed to travel to the West. He first went to Poland in March 1927 where, he was triumphantly received, and an exhibition was organised. At the end of March, he travelled further onto Berlin and later to the Bauhaus. Here, Walter Gropius, Mies van der Rohe, Hannes Meyer Lázló Moholy-Nagy and Kandinsky received him with great delight and respect. They had published his works under the title *The Abstract World*.

One of the important later paintings is his *Self-Portrait* from 1933 with the posture and in the clothing of a reformer. The hand gesture points to the missing square - a challenge to the Stalinist regime. When Malevich died in 1935, the State Russian Museum obtained the largest part of his studio. From then until 1962, no work of Malevich would be exhibited in the USSR.

The USSR had secreted away whole avant-garde collections, including those of Malevich, into the cellars. Upon the death of Lenin in 1924 at the latest, the avant-garde had lost its momentum. In 1934 under the Stalin dictatorship, Socialist Realism was extolled. Artists who did not fall into line were persecuted, arrested or deported. At the end of the 1950s, under Khrushchev and after Stalin's death in 1953, a second Russian avant-garde secretly arose, the Soz-Art (Sots Art) a combination of Pop Art and Socialist Realism. Sots Art criticised the excess of ideology in the Soviet Union and the excess consumption in the West. Among the first generation of Sots Art artists were Erik Bulatov and Ilya Kabakov.

Constructivism

Constructivism radiated a strong influence over the entire art world. Its roots are found in pre-revolutionary Russia. It used technology and the natural sciences, as well as let the newest innovations in engineering and industry steer its direction. 'Art is dead – long live the industrial art of Tatlin', was the slogan referring to the Constructivist works of this inspired inventor, Vladimir Tatlin. In his early years, Tatlin had begun

as a painter, and so, like other Russian artists, he had absorbed the innovations of French painting. His paintings from after 1910 show influences that can be traced to the works found in the Shchukin collection. Tatlin's *Female Nude* of 1913 shows references to the *Sitting Female Nude* of 1908-1909. In the course of his artistic development, Tatlin departed from the pictorially illustrated three-dimensionality of Cubo-Futurism. In 1913 he began by continuing with the spatial collages of Picasso with his three-dimensional 'constructions' made out of glass, wood, and metal. He invented the three-dimensional flying objects, the Letatlin (letat = to fly + Tatlin). One can, therefore, consider him to have laid the path for the later Action Art.

Pablo Picasso became the genius among the artists of the 20th century. Like no other artist, he made important contributions and innovations to nearly all of the artistic movements of the 20th century. He journeyed to unexplored shores and again and again produced surprising new masterpieces.

In Constructivism, pure reason and objectivity were the guiding principles. Tatlin became the antipode of all previous avant-garde movements; he became a fitting expression for the new and the world ruled by technology and the natural sciences. Tatlin tore down the barriers between the individual genres of art, between that which Art Nouveau had tried to do and Futurism had only done theoretically. Technology and utility became the absolute priority. Former followers of Suprematism like Ivan Kliun, Lyubov Popova and Varvara Stepanova were drawn to this production art form, which was conceptualised as a synthesis of the arts.

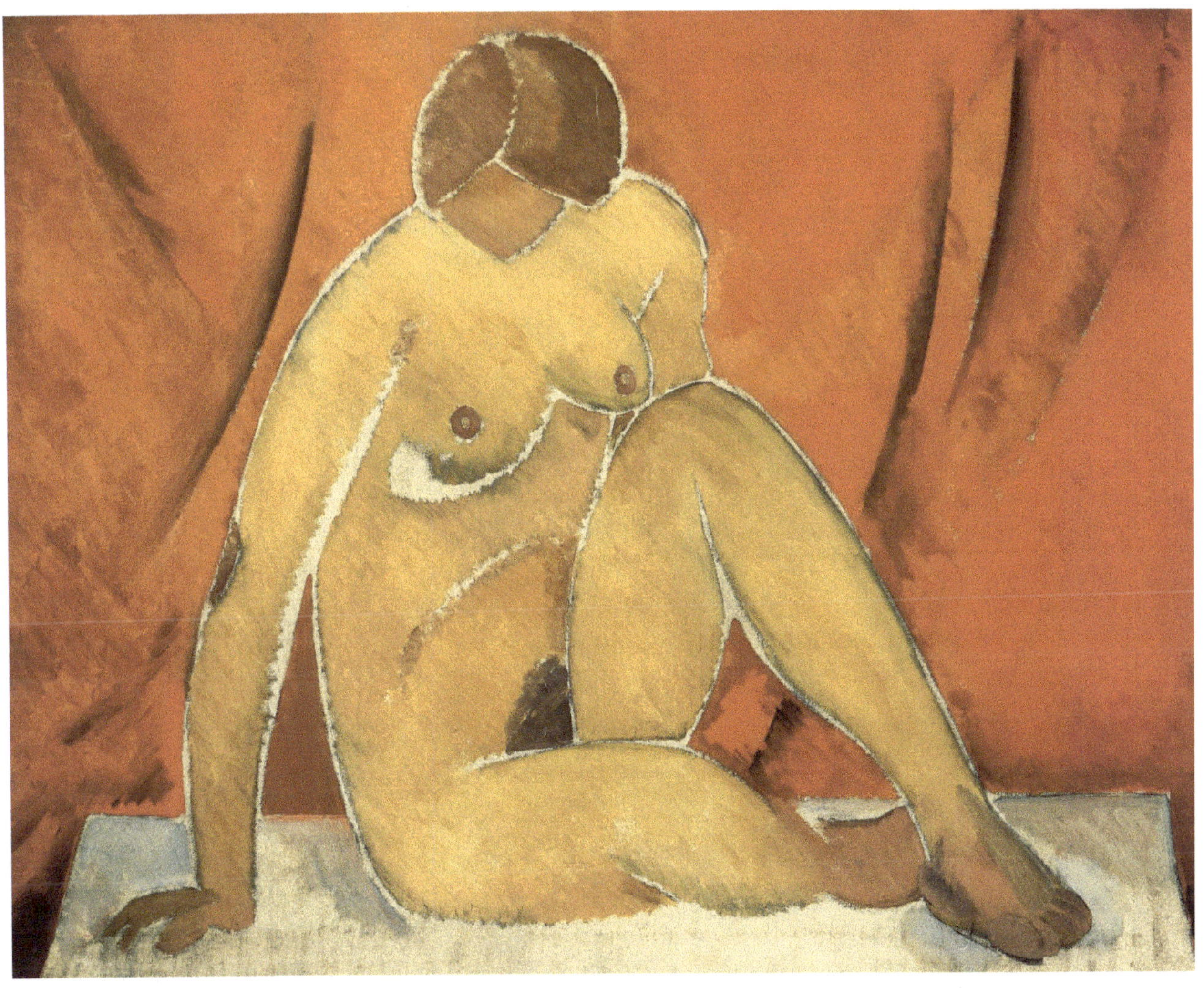

Vladimir Tatlin, *Nude*, 1910-14.
Oil on canvas, 104.5 x 130.5 cm. Russian Museum, St. Petersburg.

Alexander Rodchenko, *Red and Yellow*, 1918 (?).
Oil on canvas, 90 x 62 cm. The State Russian Museum, St Petersburg.
Art © 2007, Alexander Rodchenko Estate/Licensed by VAGA, New York, NY.

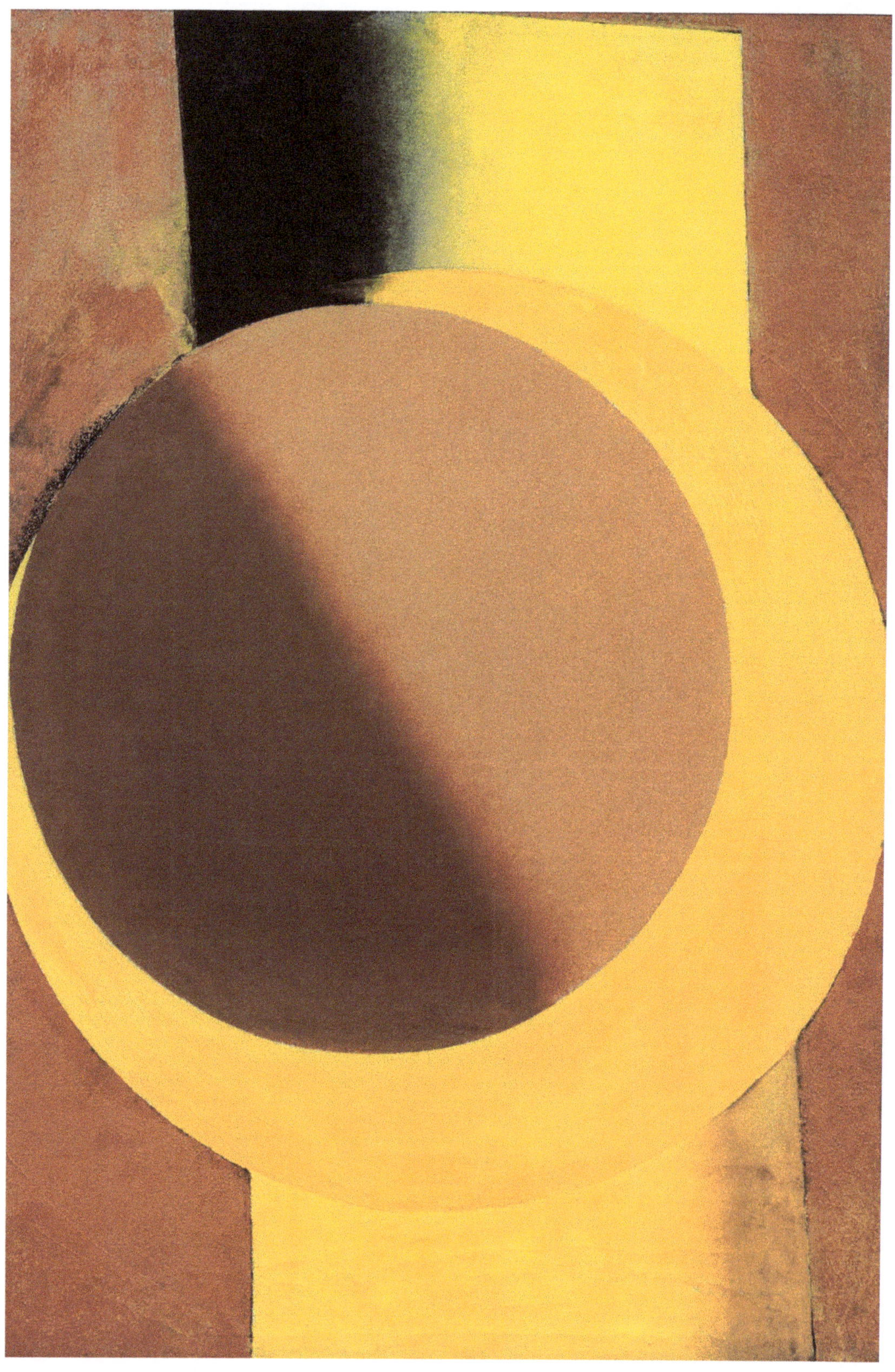

El Lissitzky, who was the director of the faculty of architecture at the State Higher Artistic and Technical Studios in Moscow, was conscious of the effect of technology. In 1919 he created the first Constructivist works. He called them Prouns, derived from the Russian Pro Unovis = for a rejuvenation of art. 'I created the Proun as a transfer station from painting to architecture. [...] It depends upon the organisation of the space by the line, plane, volume, and on their relationships and proportions.' The structure of painting, according to El Lissitzky, should be executed according to architectural laws. The shapes should be sketched out and then transferred to the canvas. Alexander Rodchenko coined the term Constructivism as the Constructivists were forming themselves into an artist group in 1921.

A short time later, Lenin announced the New Economic Policy, which only permitted art as a means of mass indoctrination. This compelled the Constructivists to retreat officially into the applied arts. Under these circumstances, Lissitzky was nevertheless able to organise exhibitions inside and outside the Soviet Union and in this way make Constructivist painters like Aleksandr Drevin, Lyubov Popova, Yury Annenkov and Alexander Rodchenko known. The first of these exhibitions took place in December 1922 at the Galerie van Diemen in Berlin. The more than 600 works of Constructivist art were met with euphoria, in particular because similar Constructivist tendencies had already developed in Poland, Hungary and Germany.

In Hungary, Alexander Bortnyik, Lajos Kassák, László Péri and László Moholy-Nagy developed Constructivist painting ideas. In Germany, Karl Peter

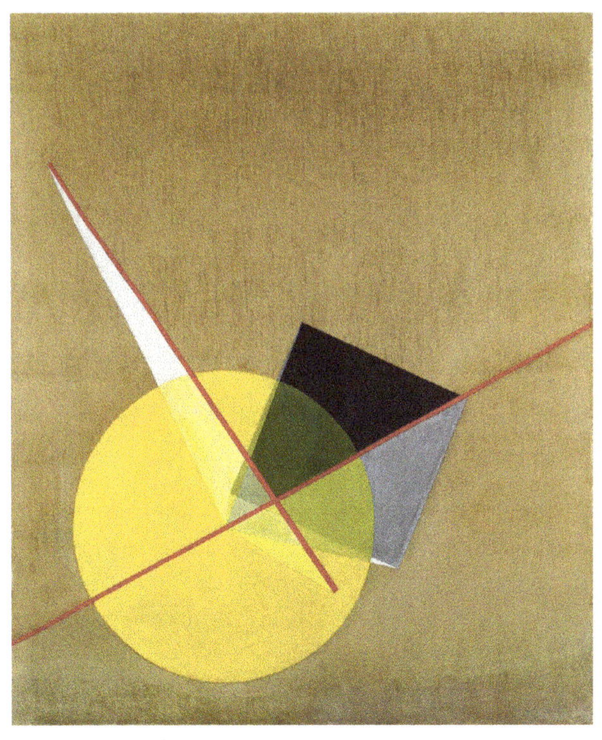

Röhl, Walter Dexel, Werner Graeff, Erich Buchholz, Carl Buchheister, Friedrich Vordemberge-Gildewart were engaged in this. Hans Richter and Viking Eggeling transferred Constructivist concepts into abstract film. In 1924 Henryk Berlewi, Henryk Stazewski and Wladislaw Strzemiñski founded the Constructivist group BLOK in Poland. The Italian, Luigi Veronesi, as well as the Belgians, Victor Servranckx and Félix de Boeck, took Lissitsky as their example.

Moholy-Nagy, *Yellow Circle*, 1921.
Oil on canvas, 135 x 114.3 cm.
The Museum of Modern Art, New York.

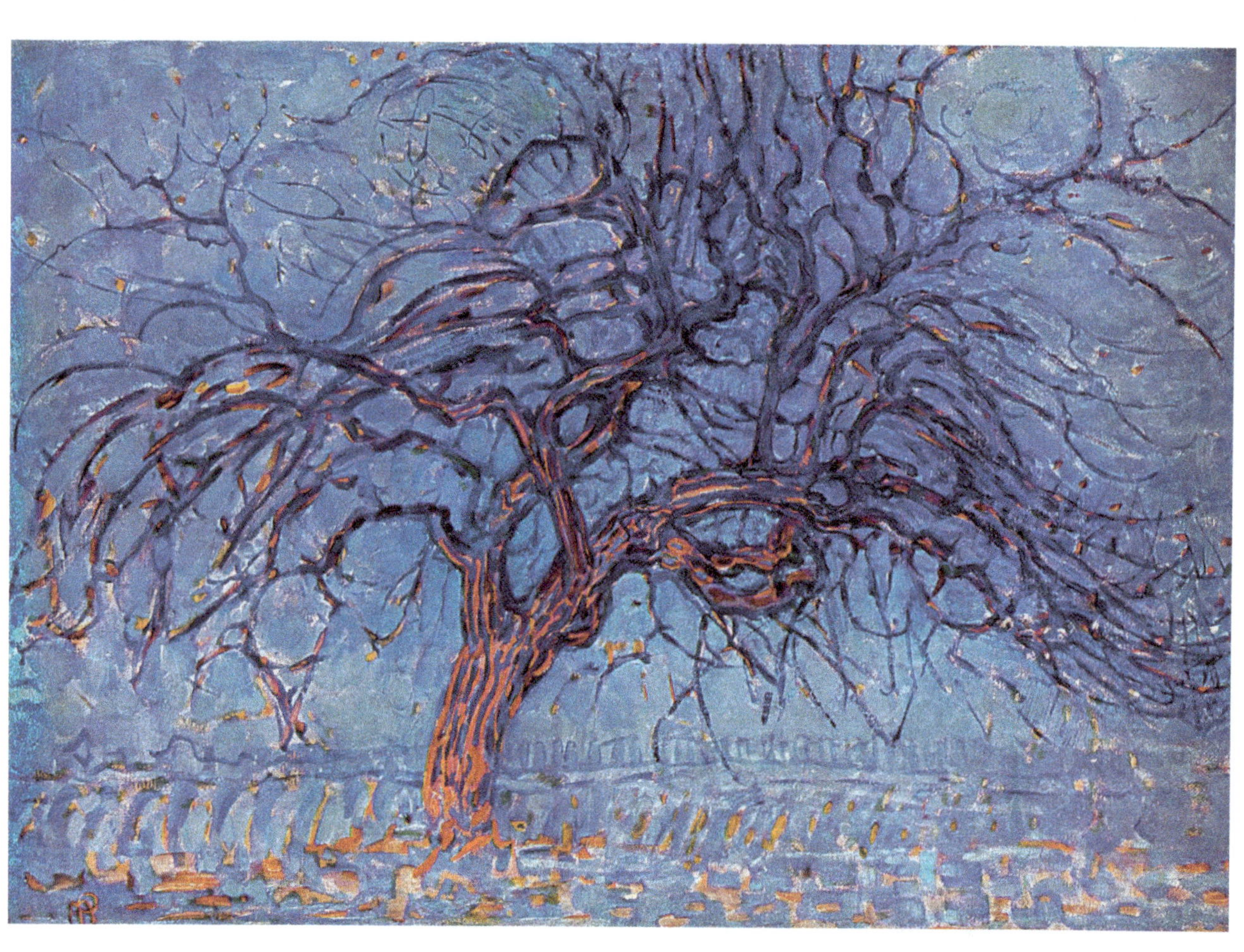

DE STIJL: THE UNIFORMITY OF THE PAINTING SURFACE

De Stijl, the Dutch counterpart to Russian Constructivism, was also oriented towards the universal and infinite. However, it was based on the theory of the Dutch theosopher, van Schoenmaeker, concerning the mathematical structure of the universe and did not have any technological visions, as did Constructivism. De Stijl, as did Russian Constructivism, entered into a dialogue with the universe, but not with technological visions as did the Russians. Rather, it did this with a philosophical-anthroposophical orientation. There are:

Two basic opposing forces that have created our earth and all earthly shapes. They are the earth's horizontal line of energy around the sun and the vertical movement of the earth rays having their origins in the centre of the sun.

Schoemaeker's teachings became the basis of the art and aesthetics of De Stijl, of which the leading mind was Piet Mondrian. He became

acquainted with Synthetic Cubism in Paris and was extremely impressed with the logic of its principles. A short time later in 1913, Mondrian sketched paintings that consisted mostly of horizontal and vertical lines.

Apollinaire coined the name Abstract Cubism for this, and this was the basis for De Stijl. During World War I, Mondrian returned home and found likeminded people there: the painter Bart van der Leck, Theo van Doesburg, Vilmos Huszár from Hungary, the Belgian painter and sculptor Georges Vantongerloo, the architects J.J.P. Oud, R. van't Hoff and Jan Wils, as well as the poet Antonie Kok. They founded the artist group, De Stijl and, at the same time in 1917, published the first issue of their magazine by the same name that ran until 1931. Later in 1925, César Domela and Friedrich Vordemberge-Gildewart joined the group. The most significant architect of the movement was Gerit Thomas Rietveld, who revolutionised architecture and design under the De Stijl banner. The first De Stijl manifesto appeared in November 1918: 'There is an old and a new time consciousness. The old one is centred on the individual; the new one is centred on the universal.' Van Doesburg explained in 1923: Our 'art is neither proletarian

Mondrian, *Evening: The Red Tree*, 1908-1910.
Oil on canvas, 70 x 99 cm.
Gemeentemuseum Den Haag, The Hague.

nor bourgeois; moreover it is gathering forces that as far as it is concerned influence the entire cultural spectrum.'

Mondrian limited the forms used in his paintings to simple geometric shapes like the straight line and the rectangle. Using the primary colours blue, yellow and red together with the 'noncolours' black, white and gray, he divided the painting surface in an uneven system of grids. With these limited formal means he wanted to create an asymmetrical equilibrium that did away with the traditional rigid and static symmetric system. The Neue Bauen (New Building) of the 1920s used these ideas, as did typography and commercial art. Some of the new ideas of De Stijl were implemented by Bauhaus. The De Stijl group broke apart in 1925. Theo van Doesburg immediately thereafter in Paris founded the Abstaction-Création group that became a refuge for more many emigrants from Germany and Eastern Europe.

Piet Mondrian was fascinated by Cubism, primarily by the drawings, when he saw it in 1911 or the first time in Paris. The black lines that were the basic element of Cubism overwhelmed Mondrian, and by 1912, he put it over the painting surface like a grille. This had the effect of the lead rods of a church window. The famous series *Trees* was created. He painted the tree again and again in progressively more abstract fashion until he had arrived at a concise form that was a sort of symbol for a tree. His studies led him in 1915 to paintings that consisted only of a pattern of vertical and horizontal lines. The amazing new thing about this was the even distribution of the symbols on the painting surface. A recognisable centre had disappeared. Now, he could draw an abstract net across the canvas, and, if he wanted, out of this series of lines, he could have the familiar resurface. The uniformity in a painting had been discovered; its complete autonomy. He sought its static strength. He found the solution for the first time in 1918 with a pure screen painting.

At the beginning of the 1920s, he composed a series of masterworks. With their large red, blue, or yellow surfaces, they radiate 90 a suggestive power of a rising, an expansion, and of dynamism in a black lattice net. Besides these, he composed works in whose centre there is a white emptiness and thereby achieves a suggestive radiating power. In the late 1930s, the all-encompassing screen paintings became prominent once again and with them the experiments with controlled coincidence. In New York, he found another item to help him with his sketches. This was adhesive tape. With this new helpful item, it became possible for him to work more quickly and to execute the random distribution of the directed shifts and regroupings more quickly. He could now avoid corrective and time-consuming repainting.

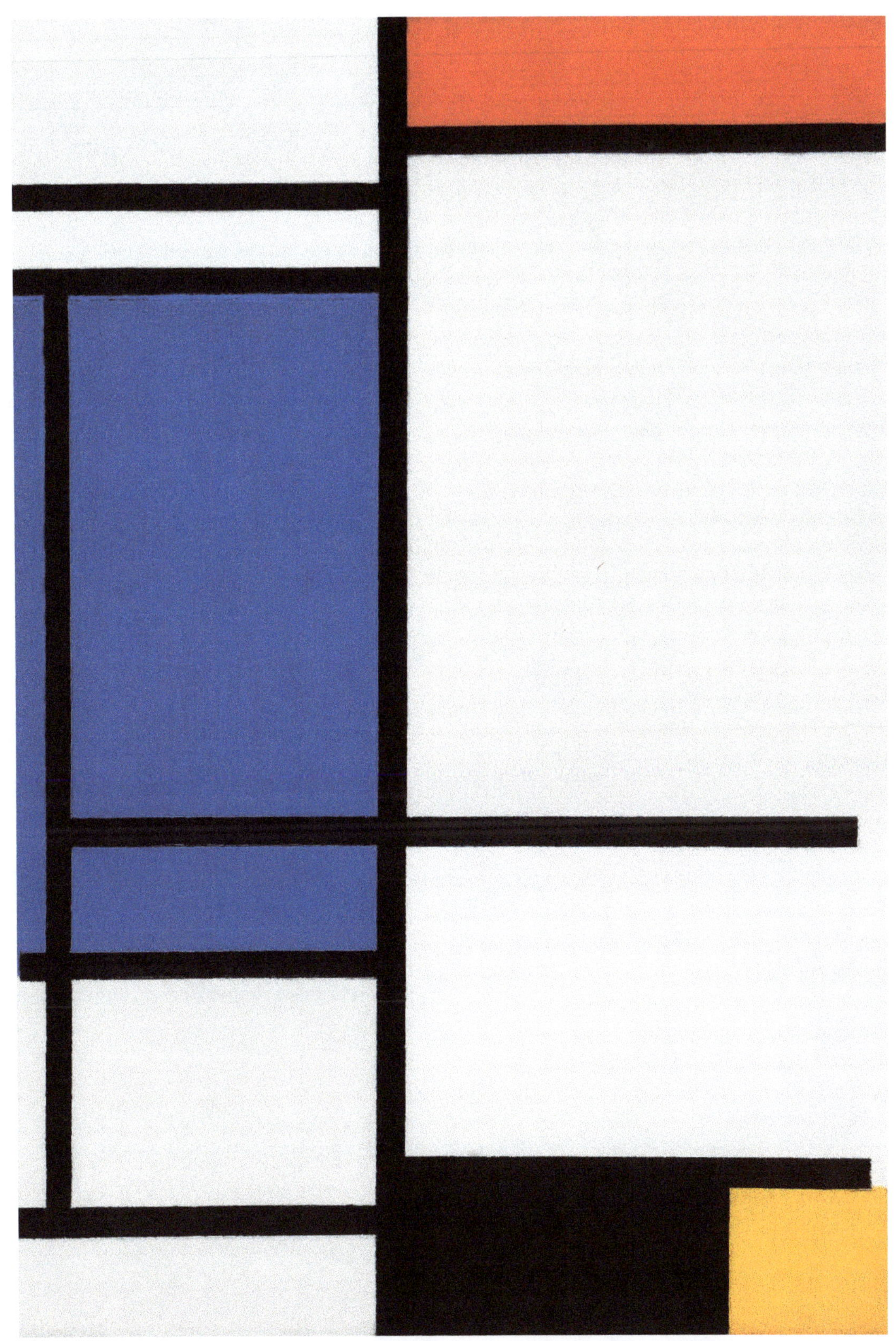

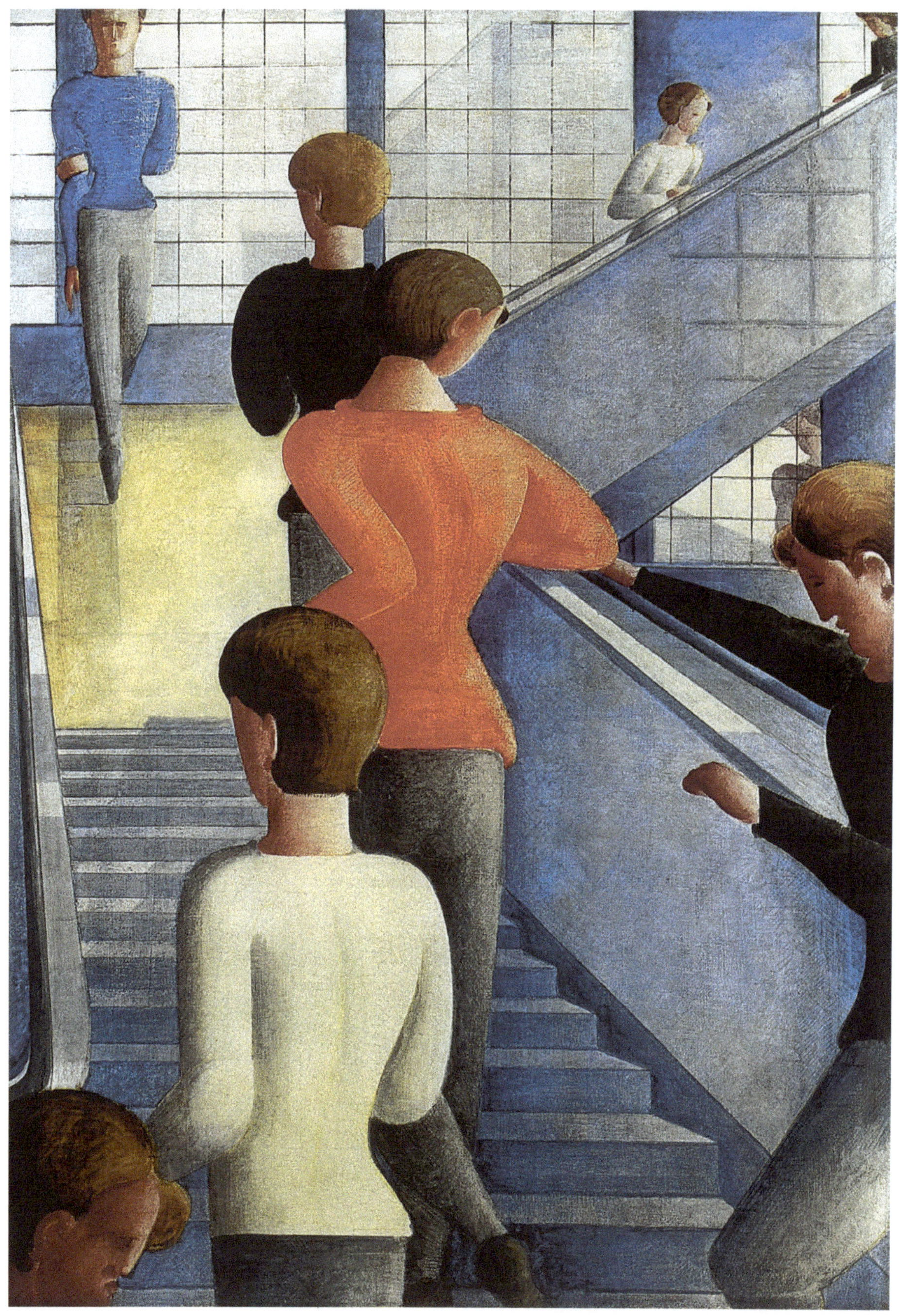

THE BAUHAUS

Rapid technical and economic growth around 1900 resulted in the creation of trade associations in many countries which, in architecture and the crafts, sought greater equality of form.

In the Bauhaus, the goals of the trades associations saw their further advancement. The medieval concept of a synthesis of the arts was re-emerging. The architect Walter Gropius founded the Bauhaus in 1919 in Weimar. Craftsmen under the direction of renowned artists, who were called 'masters', tested out fundamental ideas of shape, colour, material and their interaction. The Bauhaus wanted to put itself at the service of the industrial world and strove for the unity of all craft and artistic disciplines. Painting, sculpture, trades and applied arts were inseparable elements in the art of construction. The artist was to step out of his ghetto and work together with tradesmen and industry. Walter Gropius was successful in engaging artists with the Bauhaus who had already made a name for themselves. The aura of these individuals is the basis even today for the reputation of this school. Among the first were Paul Klee and Wassily Kandinsky, who taught in the workshops for stained glass making and mural painting. In the printing shop was Lyonel Feininger; Gerhard Marcks was in the pottery shop; and Georg Muche was in the weaving mill. Oskar Schlemmer was responsible for both wood and stone sculpture. From 1923 onwards, he was also responsible for the Bauhaus stage, following the departure of Lothar Schreyer. Johannes Itten, László Modoly-Nagy and, finally, Josef Albers taught the introductory and basic courses.

A restructuring took place after the Bauhaus moved in 1926 from Weimar to Dessau. No longer did the basic principles of Johannes Itten, stressing the sensual perception of colour and quality of materials have pride of place, but rather that of basic design. Dynamic strengths and functions of materials were tested.

In the course of their research, the Bauhaus members published diverse essays, including Josef Albers on the non-utilitarian design theory. One verified the utility of modern materials, as well as their functional and aesthetic uses. These experiments were geared towards series production, which was advantageous for industry.

Oskar Schlemmer, *Stairway of the Bauhaus*, 1932.
Oil on canvas, 162.3 x 114.3 cm.
The Museum of Modern Art, New York.

Independent, constructive thinking is required, and beyond this, the testing of uncommon materials like straw, paper, cellophane, wallpaper, corrugated board, newspaper, wire mesh, labels, razor blades ... 'Thinking is the cheapest form of wear and tear,' was the slogan. Every element had to be of equal value. Spatial thinking, new perspectives, precise observation, a most refined sense of structure, material, and for surfaces were innovations that lived on in many art genres even after World War II. The Nazis closed the Bauhaus in 1933.

The Hungarian Alexander Bortnyik opened a private studio for applied graphic arts in 1928 that became known as the Budapest Bauhaus. After fleeing the Nazi regime, Moholy-Nagy, Mies van der Rohe, Albers and Feininger founded the New Bauhaus in Chicago. In the 1950s and 1960s, their ideas influenced the Colour Field and Hard Edge painting styles in America.

In his art, Josef Albers made the reduction of shape and colour vivid with his squares. The square, as the purest of shapes, illustrates the aesthetic power of simplification. Shape in the form of a square recedes into the extreme background. The superimposition of colour layers leads to ever-new transparencies and to ever new and fascinating colour dialogues. Albers chose the nested square form so that the colour quality would appear 'free floating' and 'clearly limited' in relation to the neighbouring colours and develop a life of its own. In 1950, he began the long series *Homage to the Square* as a painting, as a silk-screen print or as a tapestry.

In 1921, the Hungarian and former lawyer, László Moholy-Nagy met El Lissitzky in Düsseldorf. He painted his first Constructivist painting, and, in the book he published in 1922 in Vienna, *Book of New Artists*, he declared his position with respect to the new art. His work at the Bauhaus from 1923 to 1928 was remarkably far-reaching. Moholy-Nagy liked to experiment and looked for new methods in new areas. So it was with coloured light, similar to Man Ray, in photograms and photomontages. And just like the brothers Gabo and Pevsner, he experimented with kinetic space modules.

Oskar Schlemmer sought the synthesis of all the arts. In the area of set design for the theatre, he could develop his ideas of harmony as a reflection of the human soul. The figure of man ought to be the measure of all things on stage as on the canvas. The preoccupation with dance and the theatre allowed him to imagine a new conception of space: space is no longer just expansion, but rather, space becomes functional; it becomes space for living. In his paintings, Schlemmer realises the imaginary space that extends itself to metaphysical concepts. The figures become distillate forms of graphic-spatial perceptions of mankind. It is a free arrangement of shapes. In the interaction of their relative sizes, they suggest a dynamic and unending spatial depth. 'With a clear imagination...cautiously and carefully,' he

Lyonel Feininger, *Gelmeroda IX*, 1926.
Oil on canvas, 108 x 80 cm.
Folkwang Museum, Essen.

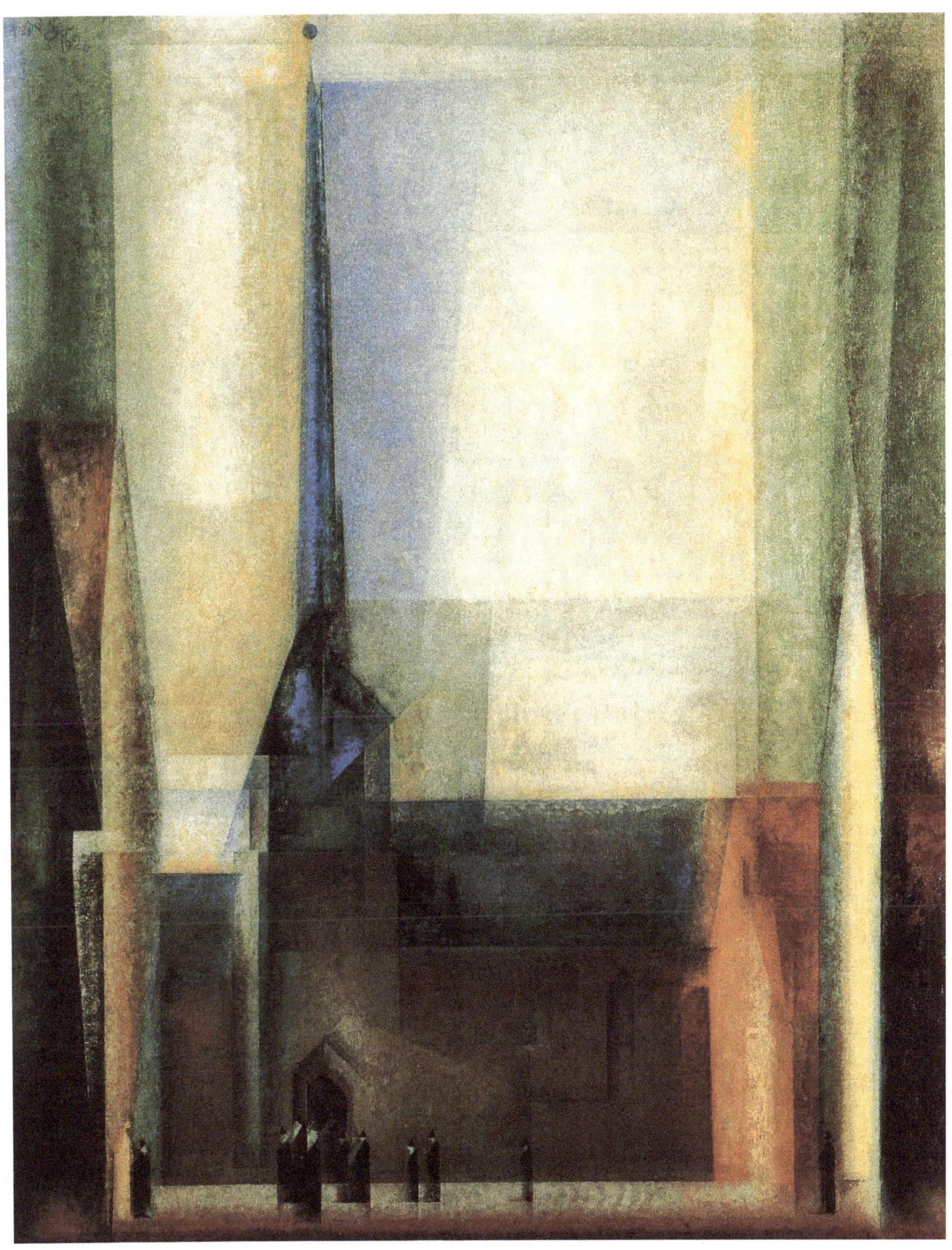

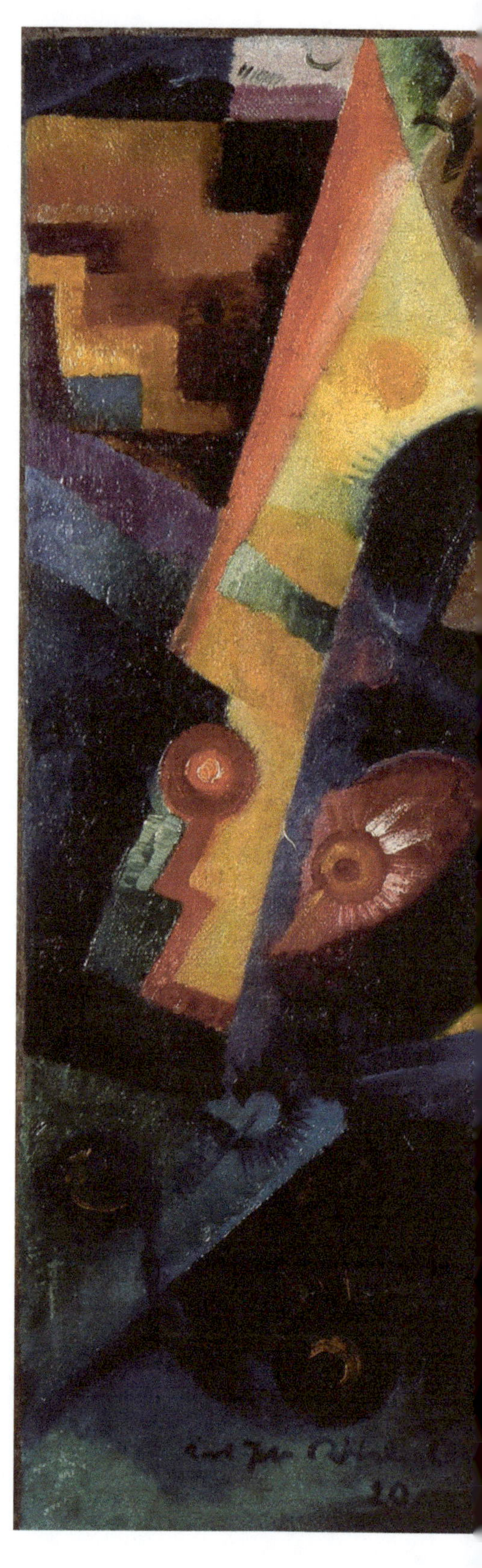

Karl Peter Röhl,
Composition with Centres of Light, 1920.

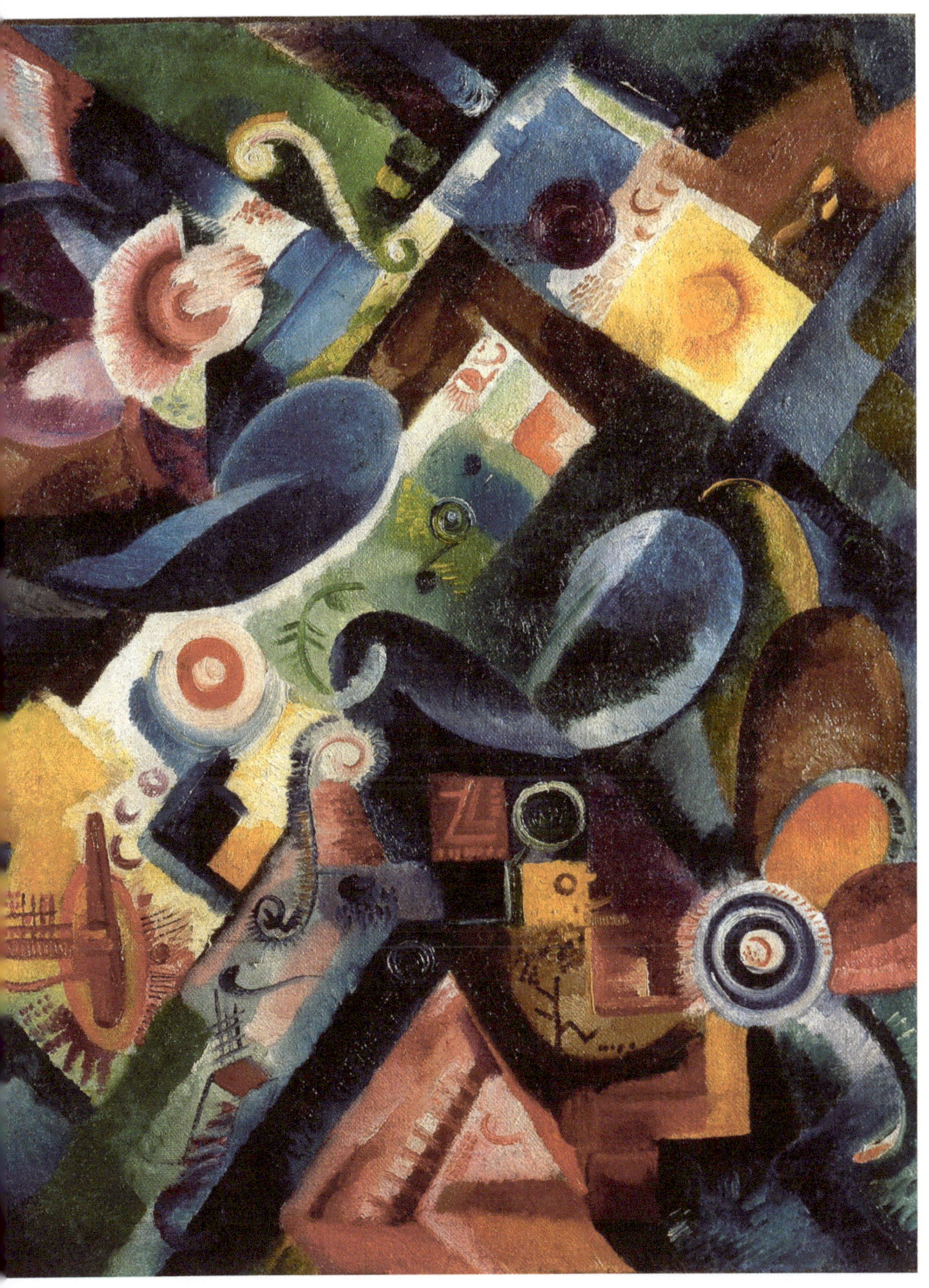

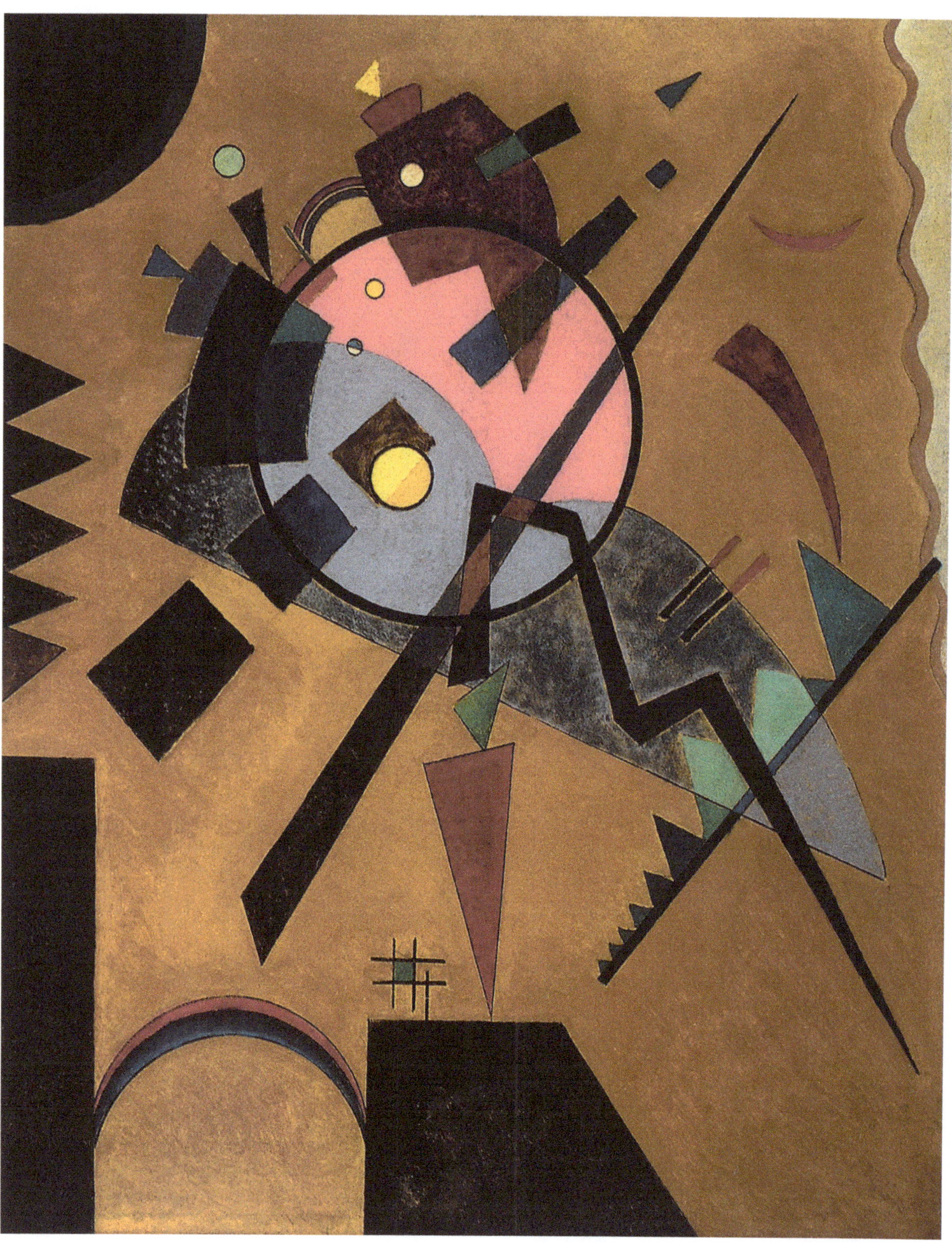

feels his way along his paintings. 'It is the thrill at the success, at the beautiful confluence of will and imagination

Lyonel Feininger's formulations of shapes and architectures pulsate with inner movement. Space, time, and motion can be captured in silhouette. Shape and space are depicted as being splintered in his early works, yet clear and precise. His compositions are filled with powerful momentum, the lines are bent and bent in angular fashion, and surfaces seem to waver within themselves, energised by a secret power. People stand as if embedded in a secret force field; the objects and the architecture interact with one another. The environment and the atmosphere, the vibrations and oscillations become noticeable; their silhouettes beat with inner movement. Their movements, those in the present, past, and those being contemplated seem as if they were implanted into the outlined shapes.

During the time he worked at the Bauhaus, Feininger's imagery became more anxious. He moved towards clear, prismatic structures, to bright, diaphanous colour planes. His transparent vision of architectural objects creates an almost immaterial world full of wide spaces and unreality. Glass-like fields of colour are superimposed and implanted into one another. Bundles of light coat the scene in the painting with crystal light. Feininger returned to America in 1937.

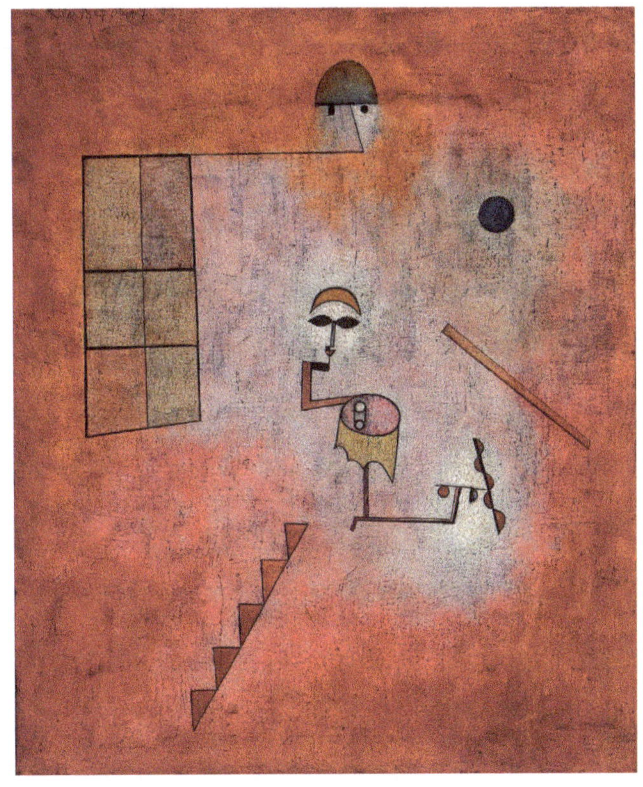

Wassily Kandinsky,
Grey and Pink, 1924.

Paul Klee,
Magic Trick, 297 (Omega 7), 1927.
Watercolour and oil on cardboard, 49.5 x 42.2 cm.
Philadelphia Museum of Art, Philadelphia.

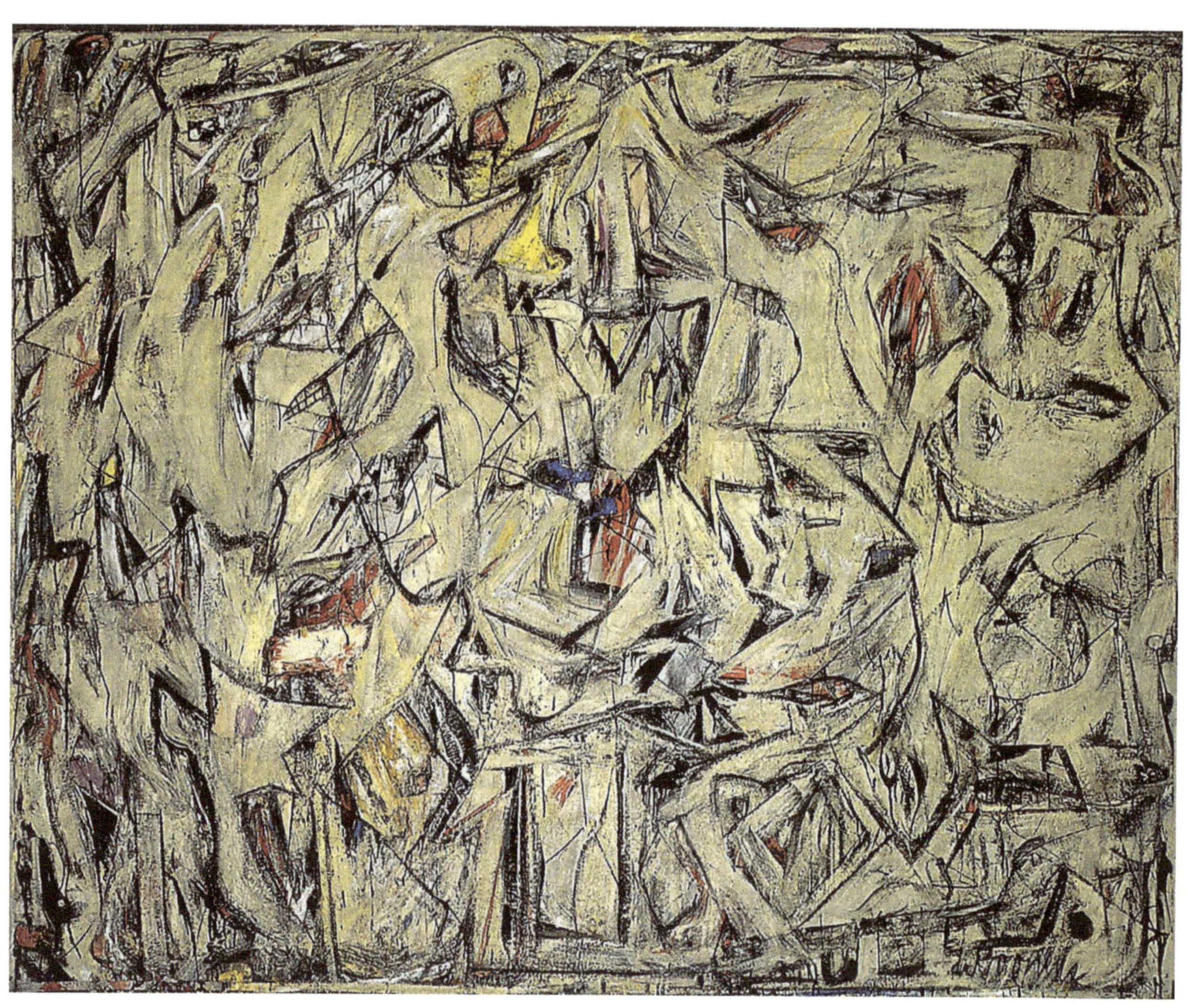

NEW YORK AND ABSTRACT EXPRESSIONISM

During the 1940s, American art took the position of world leadership with breathtaking vigour and determination. Dealers, artists, collectors, and museums began to pay increasing attention to the innovations in the American art scene. New York had become a flourishing art capital, with a constantly expanding infrastructure of galleries, art schools, and journals. There were numerous places where artists could meet. In 1943, Peggy Guggenheim, the niece of the collector Solomon R. Guggenheim, opened her exhibition space, Art of this Century. At that time, New York had only a handful of galleries. At the beginning of the fifties, there were thirty, and around 1960 about 300. The most important private art schools and hangouts for the avant-garde were the school of the painter Hans Hofmann (who had emigrated from Germany in 1933), and The Subject of the Artist, an art school where David Hare, Mark Rothko, Clyfford Still, William Baziotes and Robert Motherwell met

in 1948. Probably the most famous meeting spot for artists between 1949 and the mid-fifties was the Eighth Street Club, among whose founding members were Charles Egan, Franz Kline, Willem de Kooning, and Ad Reinhardt. Several of the artists around Abstract Expressionism were immigrants, as for example, Willem de Kooning, Arshile Gorky, John Graham, and Hans Hofmann.

In the United States of the forties and fifties, a young generation of artists came of age whose bold visions and new visual vocabulary made them the leaders of the contemporary art world. The term Abstract Expressionism, coined as early as 1919 by the author Alfred Barr in the journal *Der Sturm* and adopted by the art critic Robert Coates in his review of a Hans Hofmann show in New York in 1946, covers such different and contrasting styles as that of Mark Tobey, recalling East Asian calligraphy, the powerful colour gestures of Willem de Kooning, the passionate action paintings by Jackson Pollock, and the meditative spaces by Mark Rothko or Barnett Newman. Generally, the painters William Baziotes, Richard Diebenkorn, Sam Francis, Helen Frankenthaler, Arshile Gorky, Adolph Gottlieb, Philip Guston, Hans Hofmann, Franz Kline, Lee Krasner, Joan Mitchell, Robert Motherwell, Richard Pousette-Dart, Ad Reinhard,

Willem de Kooning, *Excavation*, 1950.
Oil on canvas, 205.7 x 254.6 cm.
1952.1, purchased thanks to Mr. and Mrs. Frank G. Logan, the Prize fund and the gift of Edgar J. Kaufmann, Jr. and Mr. and Mrs. Noah Goldowsky, Jr., The Art Institute of Chicago, Chicago.

Theodoros Stamos, David Smith, Clyfford Still, and Bradley Walker Tomlin are also counted as Abstract Expressionists, but their styles vary so much that grouping them together fails to account for the many facets of their visual language. What they had in common was the vision of a new beginning after the inhuman massacres and meticulously planned mass murders of World War II.

This second wave of abstract painting was advanced by a young generation of artists in their search for a contemporary visual language and universal values. Their spiritual sources were not, as had happened at the beginning of the century, theosophy and anthroposophy, but beliefs and rituals of indigenous people and of non-Western cultures, as well as C.G. Jung's teachings on the collective unconscious.

The early Abstract Expressionists of the New York school studied the art of Native American peoples out of a longing for historical roots and in search of universal, as well as typically American values. The spirituality of Indian culture, its basis in the mystic and ceremonial (which had been preserved unchanged through the ages) appeared to bridge the gap between indigenous and modern man, and thus could be a resource for modern life and art. The origins of this new type of abstract thinking were found, according to Barnett Newman, in the American Indian sand painting, which he first saw in Ohio in 1949: 'I was shocked by the absolute impression, the natural simplicity.'

During the 1930s, there was a growing interest in American indigenous cultures as a spiritual and aesthetic resource. Exhibitions such as Indian Tribal Arts at the Grand Central Galleries in New York in 1931, and the legendary exhibit Indian Art of the United States of 1941 in the Museum of Modern Art, as well as the outstanding permanent collections in the The National Museum of the American Indian, the American Museum of Natural History, and the Brooklyn Museum, were resources for young New York painters such as Adolph Gottlieb, Jackson Pollock, Mark Rothko, and Richard Pousette-Dart. Max Ernst and Barnett Newman also recognised the spiritual quality of the American Indian and pre-Columbian art. C.G. Jung's theory of the 'collective unconscious' added to a growing cross-cultural understanding of myth and ritual and its effects. Newman was of the opinion that primitive art was capable of providing a deeper insight into the unconscious, and that adopting such qualities would create a universal art. The totems, signs, and symbols, stemming from a long tradition in the culture of indigenous people, were only partially decipherable for the artists. Yet they knew of the transcendental, astral energies inhabiting the signs and ritual objects, and that these astral energies were emitted over periods of centuries. Each artist in his own way attempted to approach such skill, knowledge, and ability, and to incorporate it in his own work.

On 13 June, 1943, Adolph Gottlieb, Barnett Newman, and Mark Rothko published a type of

Arshile Gorky, *The Engagement II*, 1947.
Oil on canvas, 128.9 x 96.5 cm.
The Whitney Museum of American Art, New York.

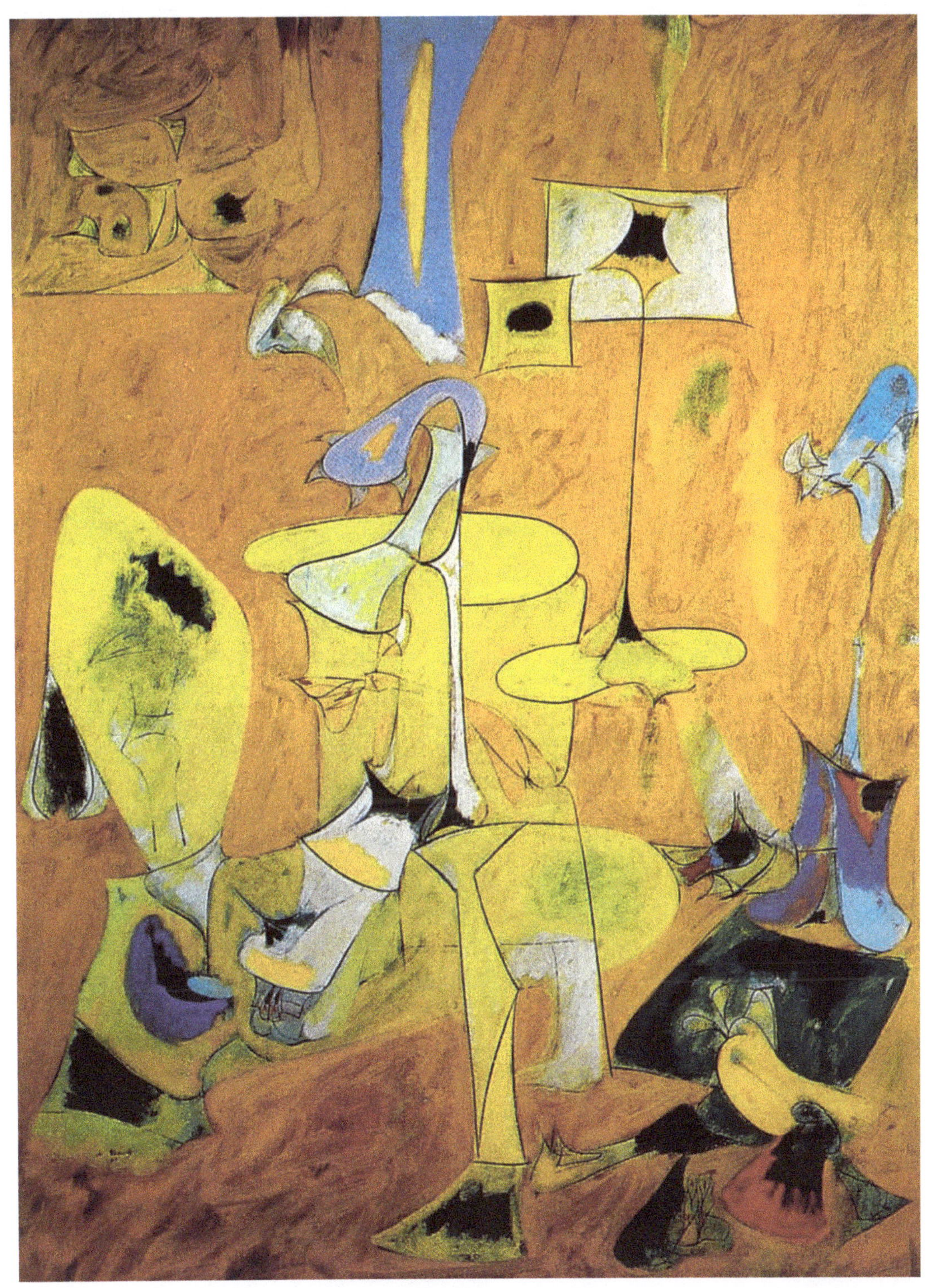

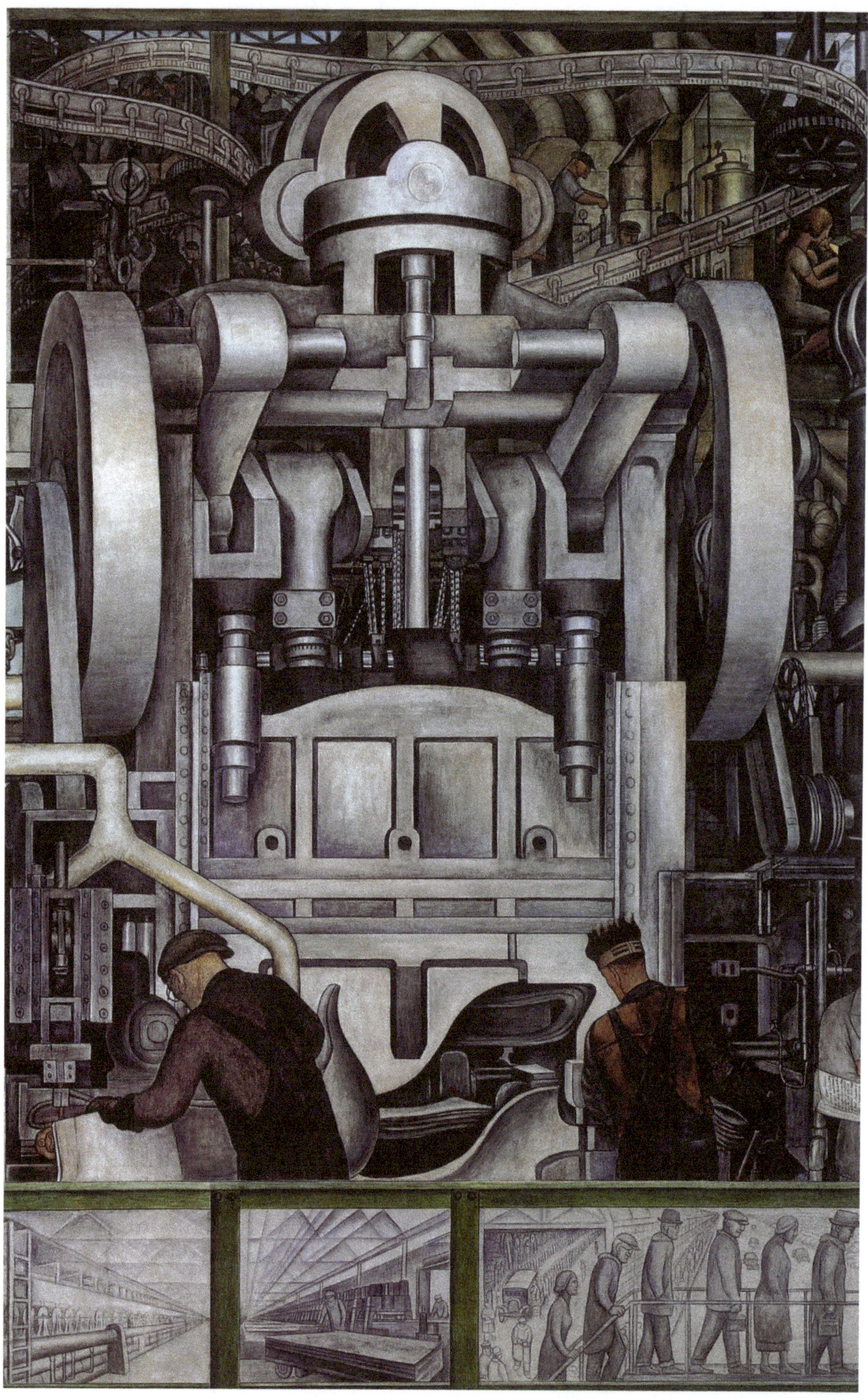

manifesto in the New York Times. This kinship the painters not only applied to the tangible sign, but specifically and emphatically to the transcendental, astral strength implicit in so-called primitive art.

Richard Pousette-Dart's encounter with indigenous art dated back to his childhood, as was the case with Pollock. In his early works he invoked the archetypical American tradition. He believed that his early works 'have an inner vibration comparable to that of American Indian art ... I feel a close kinship with the spirit of Indian art. My work stems from the spirit and the strength of America, not of Europe.' The painting *Desert*, from 1940, is a work with highly mysterious abstract ornamentation. Organic and geometric forms are connected by a strong, dark network of lines. The rough, earthen surface and structure recalls American Indian sand painters, with whom Pousette-Dart felt a close kinship.

For Adolph Gottlieb art was an expression of the unconscious. Beginning in 1941, he developed large groups of works, called pictographs, in which he makes reference to the archaic symbolic language of American Indians. *Night Watch*, painted in 1948, shows, like many of Gottlieb's paintings after 1946, a vertical structure reminiscent of carved totem poles. Mysterious androgynous creatures are outlined in simple, archaic contours. The many eyes and points have a suggestive power. These creatures give the impression of being in a

Adolph Gottlieb,
Black and Black (Burstings), 1959.

state of organic transformation. With the series *Bursts*, begun in 1956-1957, he simplified his pictorial language. In portrait format, two shapes are positioned against each other, one in the upper part of the painting, round and clearly outlined, and in the lower section another, more eruptive, undefined form. Both float before a background pointing to infinity. Each painting of the series carries another title, suggesting new ways of reading the same theme, for example, landscapes in one painting or energies in combat in another. Gottlieb is one of the few painters of Abstract Expressionism who also expressed his themes in three-dimensional objects.

Frederick Schwankovsky was Jackson Pollock's first teacher at Manuel High School in Los Angeles during the years 1925 to 1929. He was a theosophist and admirer of Krishnamurti, and suggested the concept of drip painting to Pollock. He also encouraged his other students to experiment with oil, water, colours, and alcohol mixtures, to place gigantic canvases on the floor, and to drip colour mixtures on these in order to produce stage designs such as starry skies or jungle scenes. It is probable that Pollock's experiences with colour music also stemmed from Schwankovsky, who happened to be a theoretician of colour music. For his students he published a small book which had a colour disk attached, and each colour was assigned a tone, a sign of the Zodiac, and a feeling.

The technique of dripping had also been utilised by the Mexican painter David Alfaro Siqueiros, whom Pollock had visited in his experimental

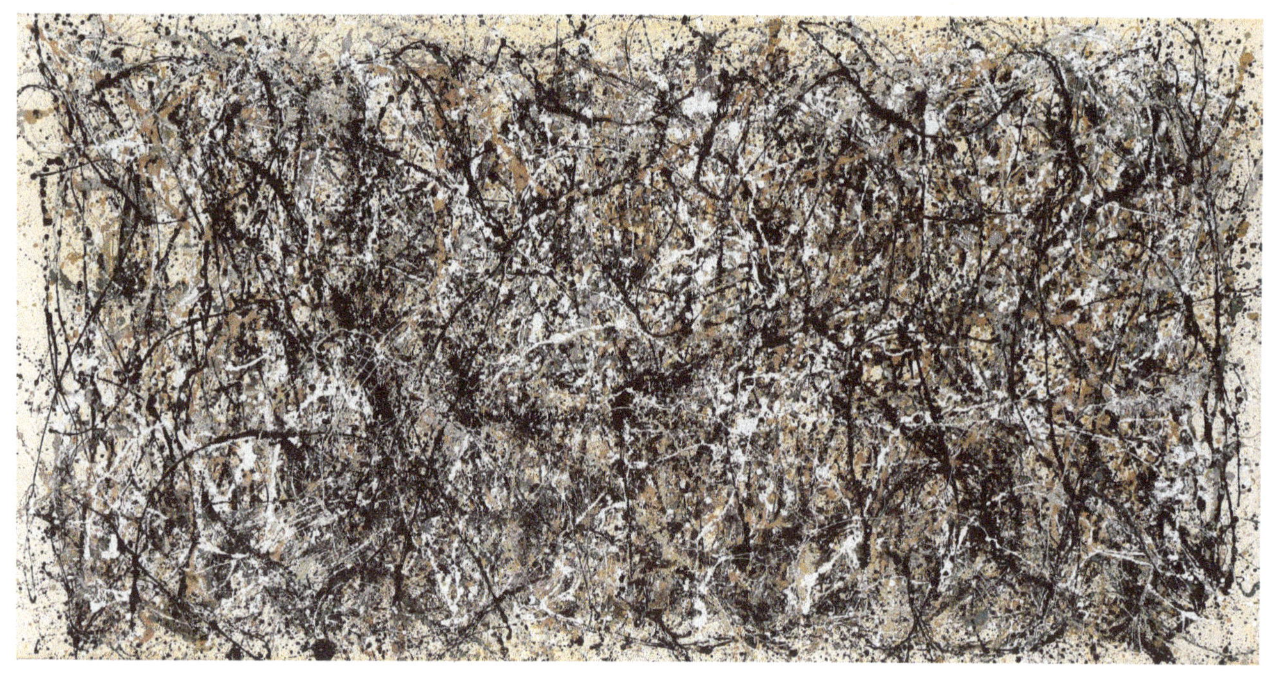

Pollock, *One. Number 31*, 1950.
Oil and enamel on canvas, 269.5 x 530.8 cm,
The Museum of Modern Art, New York.

Pollock, *Unformed Figure*, 1953.
Oil and enamel on canvas, 132 x 195.5 cm,
Museum Ludwig, Cologne.

workshop in 1936. Hans Hofmann, as well as the Surrealists Max Ernst and André Masson, had already experimented with dripping when Pollock began the drip paintings in the winter of 1946-1947. In his painting *Guardians of the Secret* of 1943, Pollock refers to masks, myths, totems, and American Indians symbols. Native American images are quoted and transformed. This painting, done before the drip paintings, is one of the most exciting as it relates to shamanism and the unconscious. The centre of the painting features a rectangle with mysterious pictograms. An agitated linear language speaks of ritual events and astral energies which these signs emit. Totem figures flank and guard the scene.

During the process of dripping, the gestures of the actor Pollock resemble those of a priest dancing. In the ritual he performs grandiose, snake-like lines. Actor, painting, and canvas merge into one. One of the typical drip paintings is *Autumn Rhythm* of 1950. The painting lives off a bold poetic gesture. All representation is abandoned. Pollock was in search of a holistic experience of nature. In this quest, the art and culture of the American Indians became a source for his re-creation.

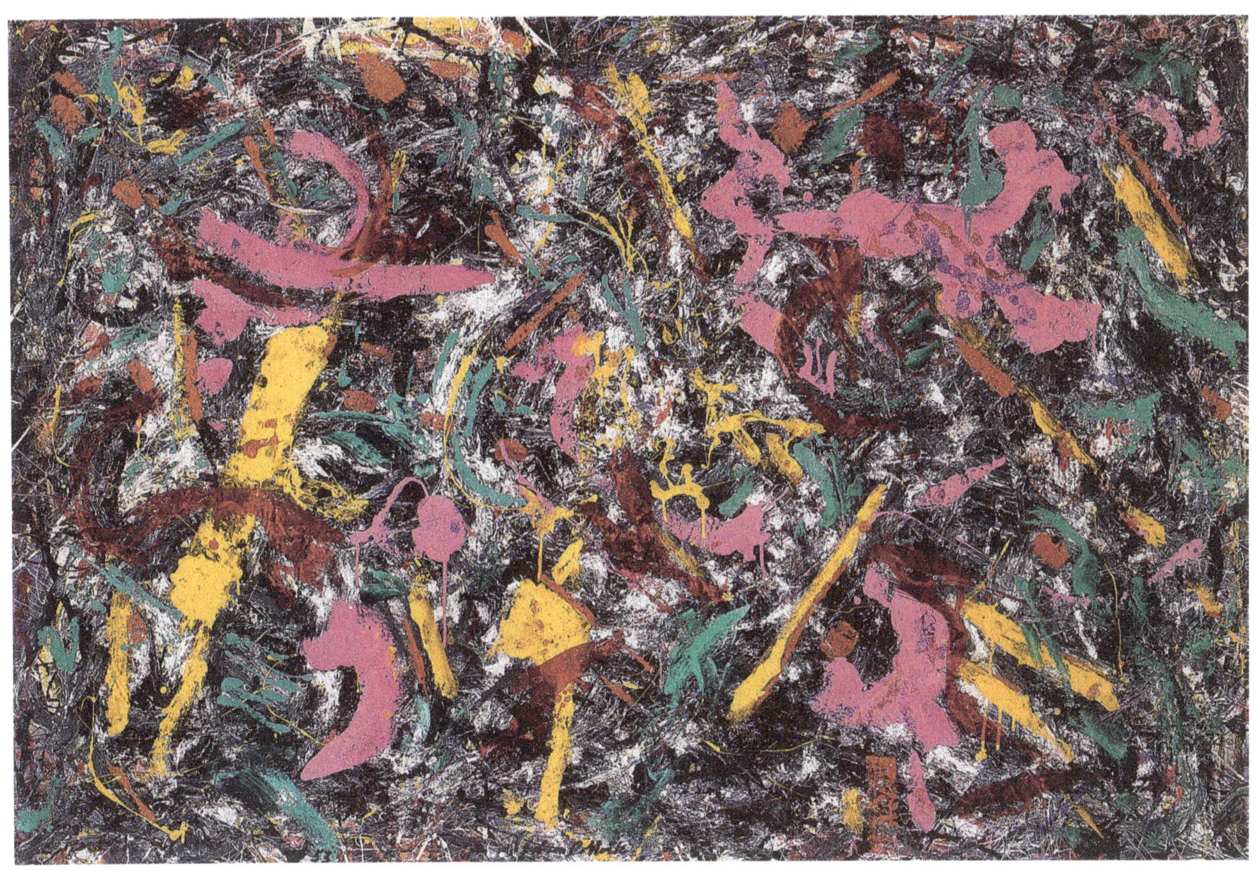

Being 'within the painting' is related to the method of the American Indian sand painters of the West. By finding himself in the painting, Pollock was not only a dancing shaman, but also the patient, who was the subject of the chanting and thus the central figure in the healing ceremony. Navajo Indians believe in the numinous power of an image. It unites the patient with nature.

The painting process called for the artist's utmost concentration in a special state of consciousness and intuitive action. Layer upon layer of the thrown and dripped paint creates a non-perspective space of incredible depth. Many of these paintings were scripts of the unconscious, written in a trance-like state. They are incredibly dense, have no beginning or end, and are endless like the universe. 'If you paint from the unconscious,' said Pollock, 'figures inevitably emerge.' This is how fantastic creatures emerge from the progression of lines, their concentration and entanglements.

Piet Mondrian always had an interest in new methods of painting. In his late creative period, in New York, where he had immigrated in 1940, he was very close to the young generation of artists and supposedly contributed to the discovery of Jack Pollock. Mondrian's art dealer Peggy Guggenheim, it is said, stood perplexed in front of one of Pollock's tangle of lines. Mondrian had told her that it was the most exciting painting he had seen in a long time.

After serious cancer surgery and an automobile accident, Arshile Gorky committed suicide in 1948. He had been friends with André Breton and the Surrealists since 1944. From his closeness to the Surrealists, he developed a style based on the observation of nature. In the summer of 1942, on his in-laws' farm in Virginia, he began to draw the movements of plants and insects in the summer heat. He developed a style which, influenced by natural powers and life-rhythms, attempted to decipher nature. This comprehensive sensual perception he transformed into a figurative abstraction. Arshile Gorky belongs to the pioneers of Abstract Expressionism.

Willem de Kooning, born in Rotterdam in 1926, arrived in New York under adventurous circumstances and without the proper documentation. Under the influence of his friend Arshile Gorky, who was of the same age, he developed a colour intensive, characteristic style of his own, vacillating between abstraction and representation. Painterly action is the focus of this multi-perspective visual language that moves between expressivity and visual construction. His language includes an immense range of polymorphic forms and expressive gestures. Occasionally, he names memories of what he had previously seen and experienced in

painting titles, such as *Merrit Parkway* or *Suburb in Havanna*. In March of 1953, he exhibited six works of his *Women* series in the renowned Sidney Janis Gallery. The theme of the human figure often appears more or less conspicuously in de Kooning's paintings. He avoided being classified as either abstract or figurative with the statement that in today's age, it might be absurd to paint a human being in colour, but that it would be more absurd not to do it. He needed to follow his impulses. These painted metamorphoses of his life experiences characterise by an eruptive style. The impression is one of being surrounded by an explosive sea of colours.

For the American Pavilion of the 1950 Venice Biennial, de Kooning created the painting *Excavation*. 'Of all artistic movements, I liked Cubism the most,' said de Kooning in 1951, and added, 'I can open nearly any book of reproductions and find a painting which might have influenced me.' Because of its large format and the reduced earthen and yellowish colours, *Excavation* indeed resembles an excavation. Like graffiti, the painting is covered by a meshwork of black lines. Signs and fragments of objects, and also of figures, appear and disappear, flash-like, in the dynamic harmony and conflict of a

Mondrian, *Composition of Lines and Colour: III*, 1937.
Oil on canvas, 80 x 77 cm.
Gemeentemuseum Den Haag, The Hague.

Pollock, *Alchemy*, 1947.
Oil on canvas, 114.3 x 221 cm,
The Peggy Guggenheim Collection, Venice.

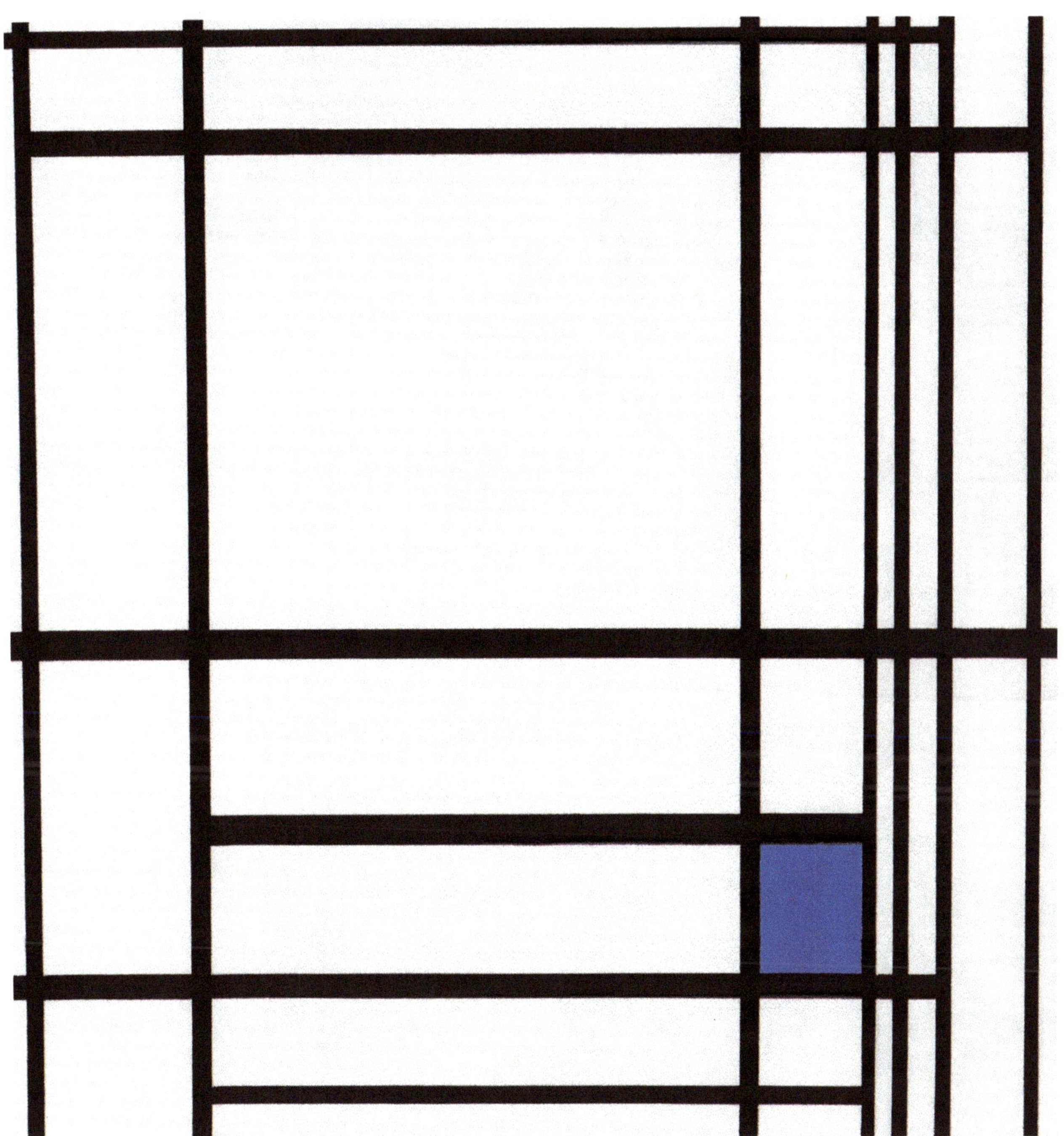

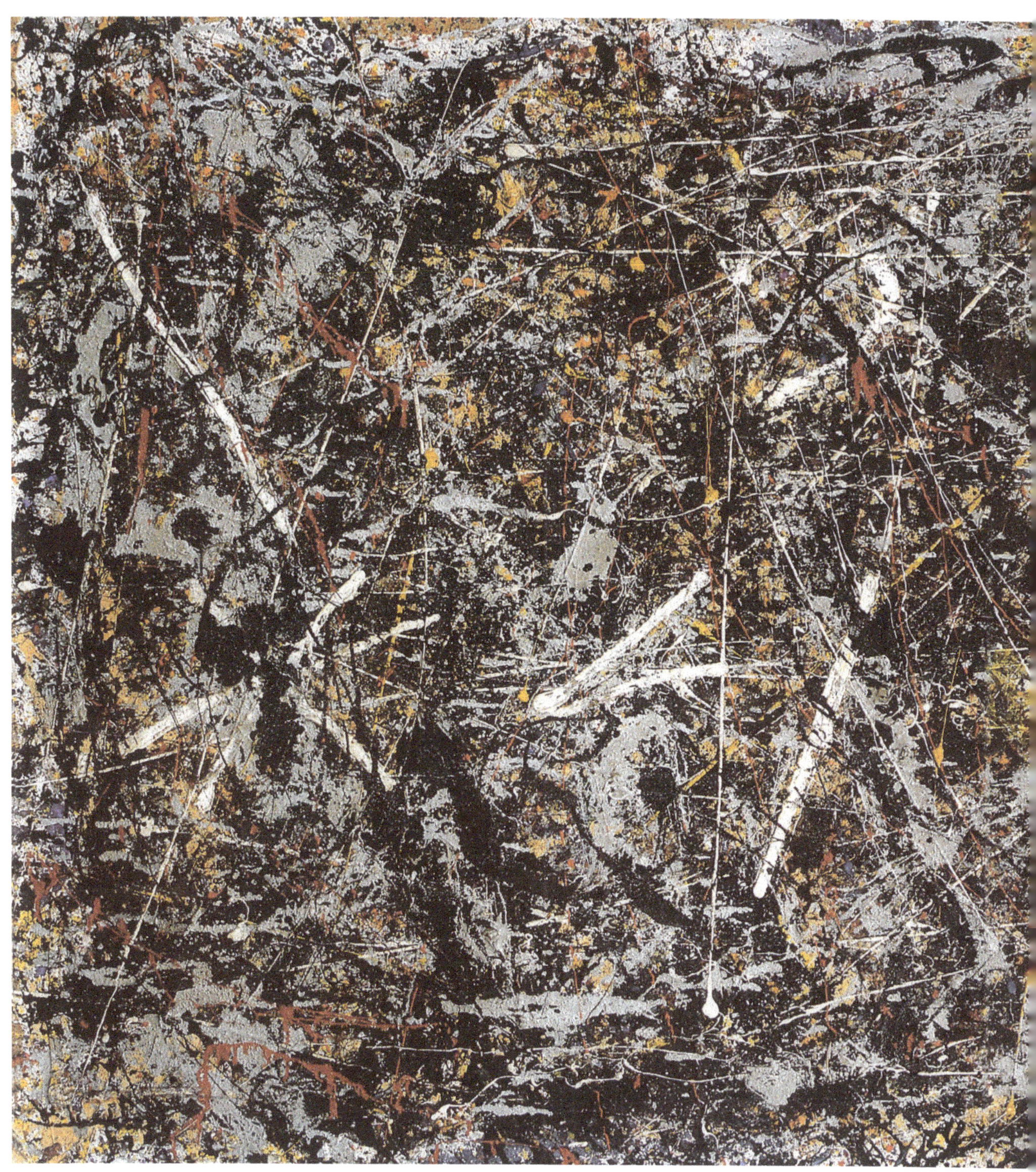

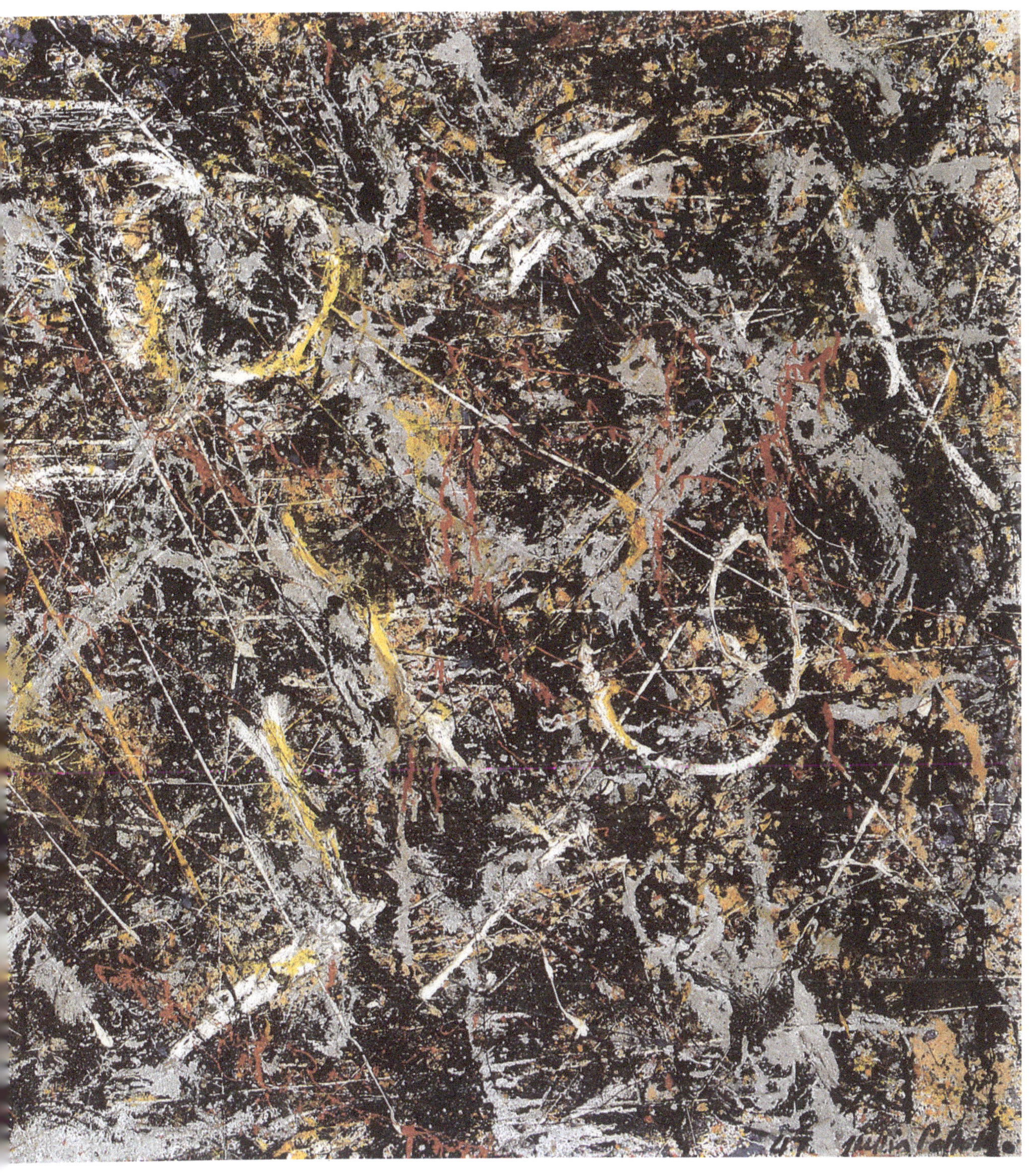

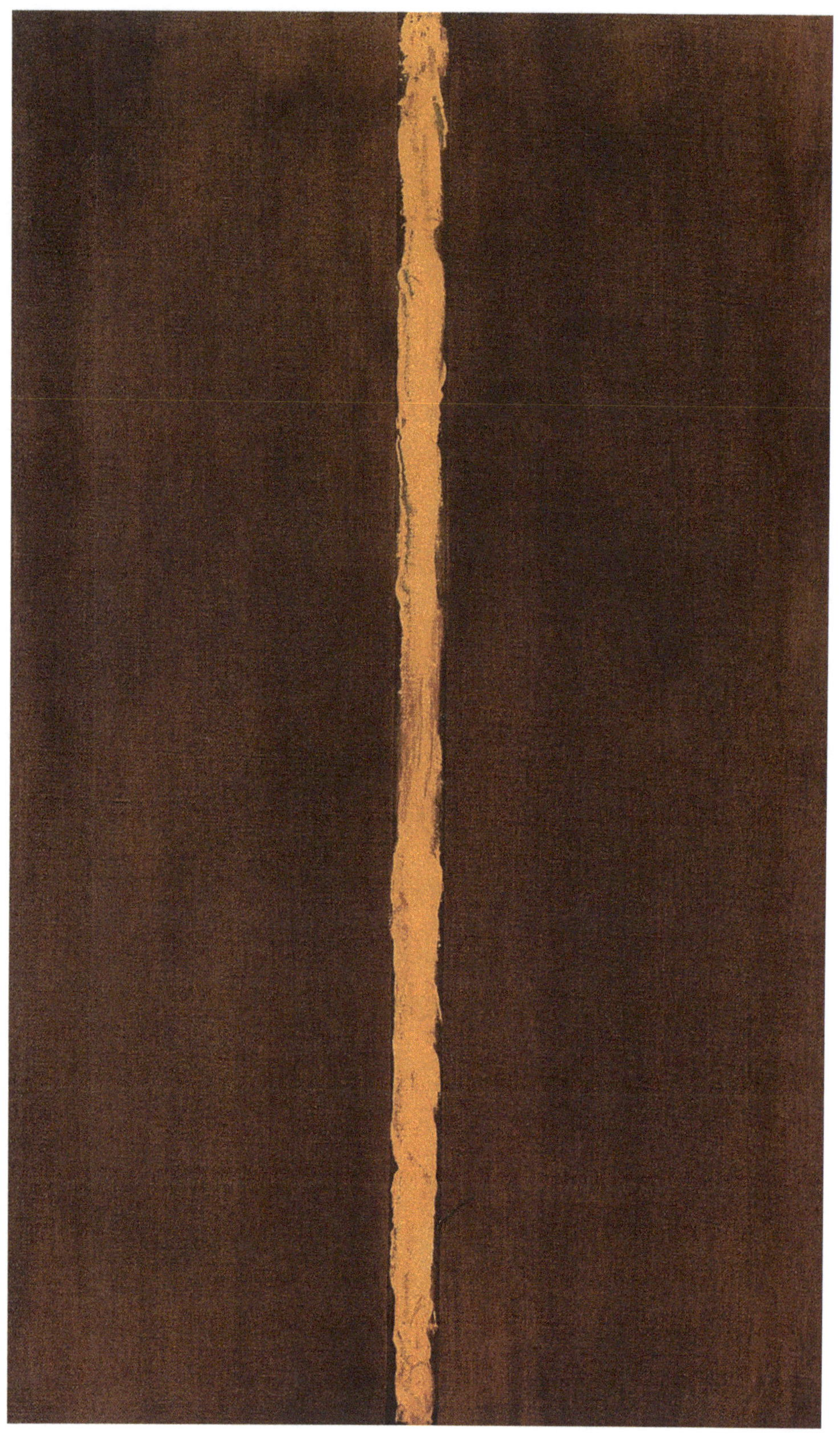

tumultuous scene. The artist paints an energy-laden process of tension and release, of comings and goings, a multi-lingual hullabaloo. For this painting de Kooning was awarded the 1951 Purchase Prize of the Art Institute of Chicago. Immediately after finishing *Excavation*, de Kooning began the *Women* series.

Franz Kline's work is characterised by powerful gestures in black and white. Only in his later works does colour enter the paintings. His thick black lines painted with the verve of Action Painting imply pent-up energy. As symbols of power, the black beams extend across the large-format canvases. White paint provides background for the vehement black agitation. His paintings often appear like landscapes seen from very far above, which the artist underscores by occasionally naming places and railroads in his titles. The painting process often extended over weeks. Also, Franz Kline often worked on several paintings simultaneously. He frequently worked from sketches which he had spontaneously drawn on newspaper or pages of telephone books.

Barnett Newman painted his *Onement I* in 1948. It marked a turning point in his artistic development. Many years later Newman commented on the painting: 'I recognised that

Barnett Newman, *Onement*, I, 1948.
Oil on canvas and oil on adhesive tape on canvas,
69.2 x 41.2 cm. Gift of Annalee Newman,
The Museum of Modern Art, New York.

I had made a statement that touched me and that constitutes the beginning of my present existence, because from that point on I had to abandon any connection to the experience of nature.' *Onement I* is a reddish-brown painting in portrait format. An orange-coloured, variegated adhesive tape divides the canvas into two halves. The vertical strip, which Newman called a 'zip,' separates and at the same times unites both parts of the painting like a zipper. Newman commented: 'A field, which perks up the other fields, just as the other fields perk up this so-called line.' *Onement I*, which had gained a status of its own, now had an existence of its own. In the following year, Newman created 17 similar compositions. The dimensions grew, so as to increase the physical difference in the polarity between painting and viewer. The invention of the zip depicts what Newman in 1945 called the 'metaphysical problems of part and entity ... where man is on his own, alone, and lonesome, and yet he belongs somewhere, is part of another. This conflict is our biggest tragedy.'

Between 1956 and 1957, Newman experienced a creative crisis. In November of 1957 he suffered a heart attack. Three months later, he began a cycle of fourteen variations on a theme, which he later called *Stations of the Cross – Lema Sabachthani*. With this cycle, Newman created his master work. Art historian Franz Meyer even went so far as to call it the 'Sistine Chapel of the 20th century.' Only during the process of painting did the artist himself realise the deep reaching, universally true, as well as autobiographic dimension of these new works.

Newman spoke of astral energies which he himself had put into the painting and which now, released and come to life, gave the paintings the timeless transcendental strength characteristic of masterpieces. The viewer who falls under their spell is able to read them.

This was not meant literally. Rather, each Station was to offer a pictorial representation of the artist's emotions and physical existence during the creative process. Each *Station of the Cross* was to be a conglomerate of a segment in his life. The artistic means he chose are extremely sparse. With the colours black and white, as well as with non-primed canvas and adhesive tape, he created a comprehensively textured, universally valid image of life and world: a universe.

While Barnett Newman's work is defined by the vertical line, that of Marc Rothko is defined by colour, which can continue beyond the edge of the painting into infinity. Rectangular fields of colour, whose edges seem to dissolve, float before a light background. His 'icons' which hide more than they reveal, draw the viewer into an expanse of light, hinting at the presence of an invisible God who, according to the Jewish religion, may not be represented figuratively. Like temple curtains, the colour fields with their runny edges cover what is behind them, the large emptiness, infinity. Rothko was of the belief that beside visible reality there is a world which generates the consciousness of man, as well as one, also created by God, which is beyond human consciousness. His paintings were, to him, independent, autonomous unities which mirrored the 'laws and basic needs of all that is alive.'

Rothko created his last large group of works, the Rothko Chapel in 1965-1966. This was commissioned by the collectors Dominique and John de Menil. The non-denominational Rothko Chapel was built according to the artist's concepts in the heart of museum district in Houston, Texas. Beginning in 1957, Rothko's works had taken on an increasingly darker colour scale, in, as he put it, 'an obvious occupation with death.' These nocturnal paintings possess an aesthetic severity. The harmony between architecture and painting adds to this impression, as does the glaring sunshine of the south-western United States. All fourteen canvasses of the series he painted in dark colours, including the three triptychs. Monochrome paintings alternate with paintings whose colour fields are for the first time bordered by hard edges. The chapel was inaugurated posthumously in 1971. For the exterior, in 1967 Barnett Newman created the *Broken Obelisk*.

'I am in search of a unified world in my paintings, and am employing a constant swirl in order to accomplish this.' Mark Tobey has become known as the painter of Colour Field paintings, whose surface is covered by a tightly woven network of lines by simple structures in rhythmic symmetry,

without centring or accentuating. They claim to continue beyond the frame of the canvas into infinity.

In 1935, after a stay at a Zen monastery near Kyoto, Tobey began his series of *White Writing*s. They call for meditative contemplation. Occasionally, titles such as *Radiant City* evoke visions in the viewer, such as when the delicate web of lines turns into lights flickering above a city.

Ad Reinhardt, the painter of *Black Paintings*, categorically excluded any references to representation in his paintings. Beginning in 1954, he reduced his geometric visual language to black and broken tones of black. He forced himself to be as objective as possible and to wipe out any traces of a personal style. His purist works, nevertheless, do manifest an individual style by reducing the colour scale to black, thus providing an impenetrable surface. The surface is dull, to avoid reflection and penetration into its blackness. Reinhardt leads the viewer to the limits of what is visible. Square and rectangular patterns of hardly recognisable tonal differences - he added a bit of brown, green, or blue to black to minimally structure the surface. His works are to be understood in the context of the European development of Concrete Art, of Josef Albers and his 'homage to the square,' of Yves Klein's monochrome paintings, and in the context of the pioneers of abstraction, Cubism, of Mondrian and De Stijl, of Malevich and Suprematism.

Ad Reinhardt, *Abstract Painting, Red*, 1952.
Oil on canvas, 274.4 x 102 cm.
The Museum of Modern Art, New York.

Yves Klein, *No Title, Blue Monochrome*, 1959.
Synthetic resin with dry pigments on canvas fixed on wood, 92.1 x 71.8 cm.
Guggenheim Museum, New York.

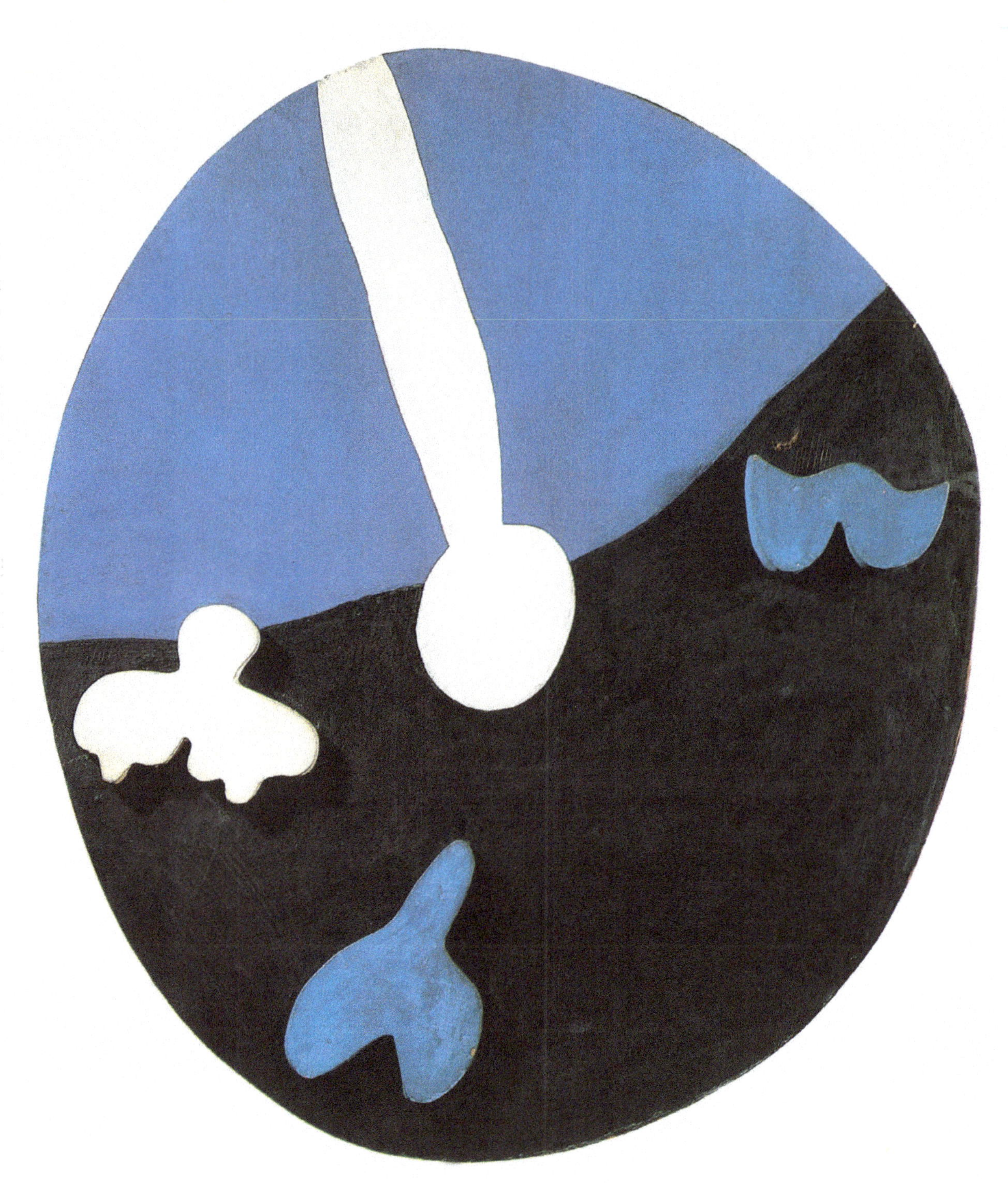

EUROPE AND ABSTRACT EXPRESSIONISM

After World War II, the great period of Abstract Expressionism also reached Europe. This new style, without rules or formalism, meant freedom from any doctrine. Emotions could be spontaneously realised on the canvas, without having been filtered or channelled in any way. In the United States, Abstract Expressionism met with existing styles, and together with these, it extended to South and Central America, as well as Japan. Europe, like the United States, developed a multitude of variations, including Art Informel, Tachism, and Lyrical Expressionism. The empathetic gesture, improvisation, the spontaneous, subjective expression were also a move away from the reality of the past, a flight from the awareness of the cultural darkening and the impoverishment of art during the period of National Socialism.

Turning toward spirituality, as well as to the inner self, appeared the best solution in this misery. And when, during the mid-fifties, Socialist Realism became the officially sanctioned style in countries such as Eastern Germany or other countries in Eastern Europe, abstraction once again advanced noticeably as the artistic expression of the free, democratic world.

In Europe, with its rich traditions, one could draw back on the achievements of the avant-garde at the beginning of the century, the great role models for this new concept, such as Kandinsky, who at the beginning of the century had already tried to have stirrings of the unconscious enter the painting.

Documenta I in Kassel in 1955 showed a retrospective of European art in context, from Classical Modernism to the beginnings of the new West German developments. In addition to artists such as Hans Arp, Henry Moore, and Pablo Picasso, some West German artists were included, such as Karl Hartung, Hans Uhlmann, Ernst Wilhelm Nay, and Bernhard Heiliger. The young generation of artists, however, was already exploring new ways of perception and creation.

Hans Arp, 1886-1966, *Dada, French, Clock*, 1924.
Painted Wood. Private collection.

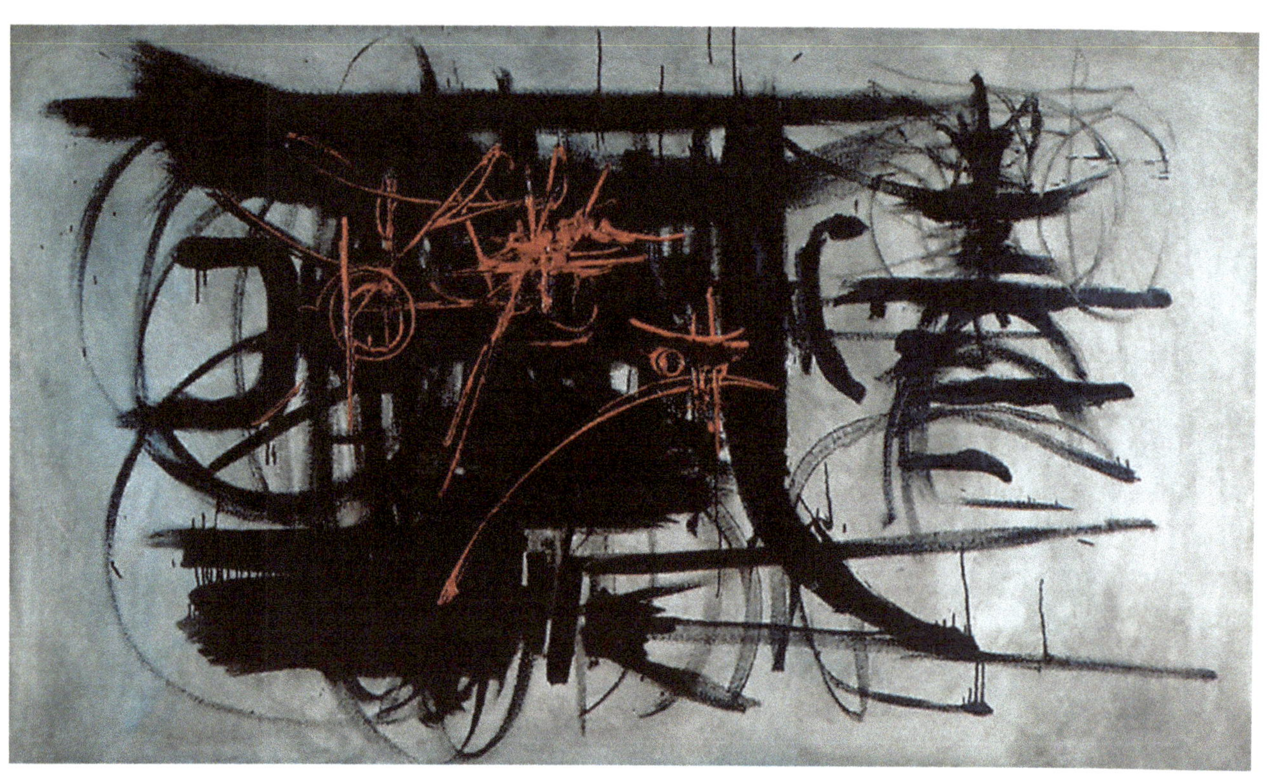

ÉCOLE DE PARIS AND TACHISTS

etween 1945 and 1960, many of the abstract artists were associated with the École de Paris. Roger Bissière, who previously had been part of the Cubist school, painted floating grids of small frames in colour. Nicolas de Staël applied his expressive colours to the canvas with a palette knife, not by brush: 'One paints in a thousand vibrations the blow which one perceives.'

Pierre Soulages preferred deep black since he wanted to renounce the 'loquaciousness of colour' in favour of the spiritual black. Georges Mathieu, the artist who painted with great speed, defined his very rapid calligraphic improvisations solely as a psychological process.

In mid-1947, Mathieu saw works by Wols (Alfred Otto Wolfgang Schulze) in the Parisian Galérie Drouin and recognised their mastery: 'Each is more crushing, more disturbing, more bloody than the other: an event, no doubt the most important since the works of Van Gogh.' Wols, who had been living in Paris since 1932, blurred his images with

turpentine. From a certain point on, he intervened to give direction. Wols fixated the process of painting from the unconscious with brush strokes and scratched lines.

Hans Hartung, who had lived in France from 1935, wrote graphic 'psychological profiles' full of dynamism and emotion. The poet and painter Henri Michaux, formerly a student of at the Bauhaus, used experiments in states of intoxication for his fantastic-surreal abstractions. Jean Bazaine, Camille Bryen, Maurice Estève, Maria Manton, Jean le Moal, Antonio Saura, Maria Helena Vieira da Silva, Gustave Singier, Emilio Vedova, Alfred Manessier, or Helen Frankenthaler, all created a wide range of gestural painting, from L'Art Informel via Abstract and Lyrical Expressionism all the way to Tachism.

In France, the term Tachisme was preferred. The patches of colours (taches=stains) were applied freely and without predetermination to the canvas. The result depended solely on the impulse of the moment and the choice of colour and material. The gesture had a purpose. It was a clear system of communication and a comprehensive structure in the canon of place and time. The spontaneous act of painting, taking into account the unconscious, was merely a reference to

Georges Mathieu, *Guibert de Nogent's Silence*, 1951.
Oil on panel, 130 x 217.5 cm.
Musée National d'Art Moderne,
Centre Georges Pompidou, Paris.

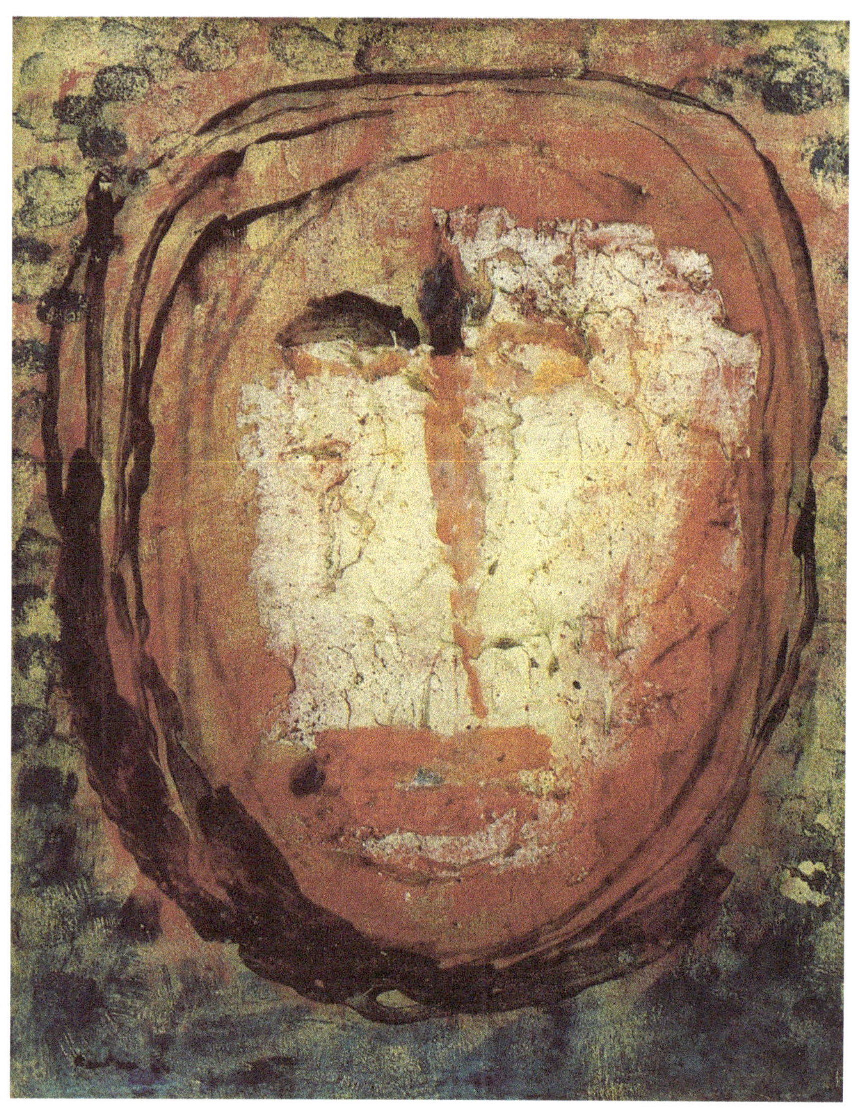

Jean Fautrier, *Hostage's Head No. 2*, 1943.
Private collection, Paris.

Jean Dubuffet, *The Road of Humankind*, 1944.
Oil on canvas, 129 x 96 cm.
Gift of Ludwig, Museum Ludwig, Cologne.

the painting process, not to the content of the works. The painters of L'Art Informel were once again in search of spontaneity without the rules of civilisation. The philosophical basis for the intuitive and meditative method of painting was the existentialism of Husserl, Sartre, Heidegger, and Kierkegaard, as well as Indian and Zen-Buddhist philosophy. A fresh sign language, new methods of painting, and an impasto application of paint were some of its variations.

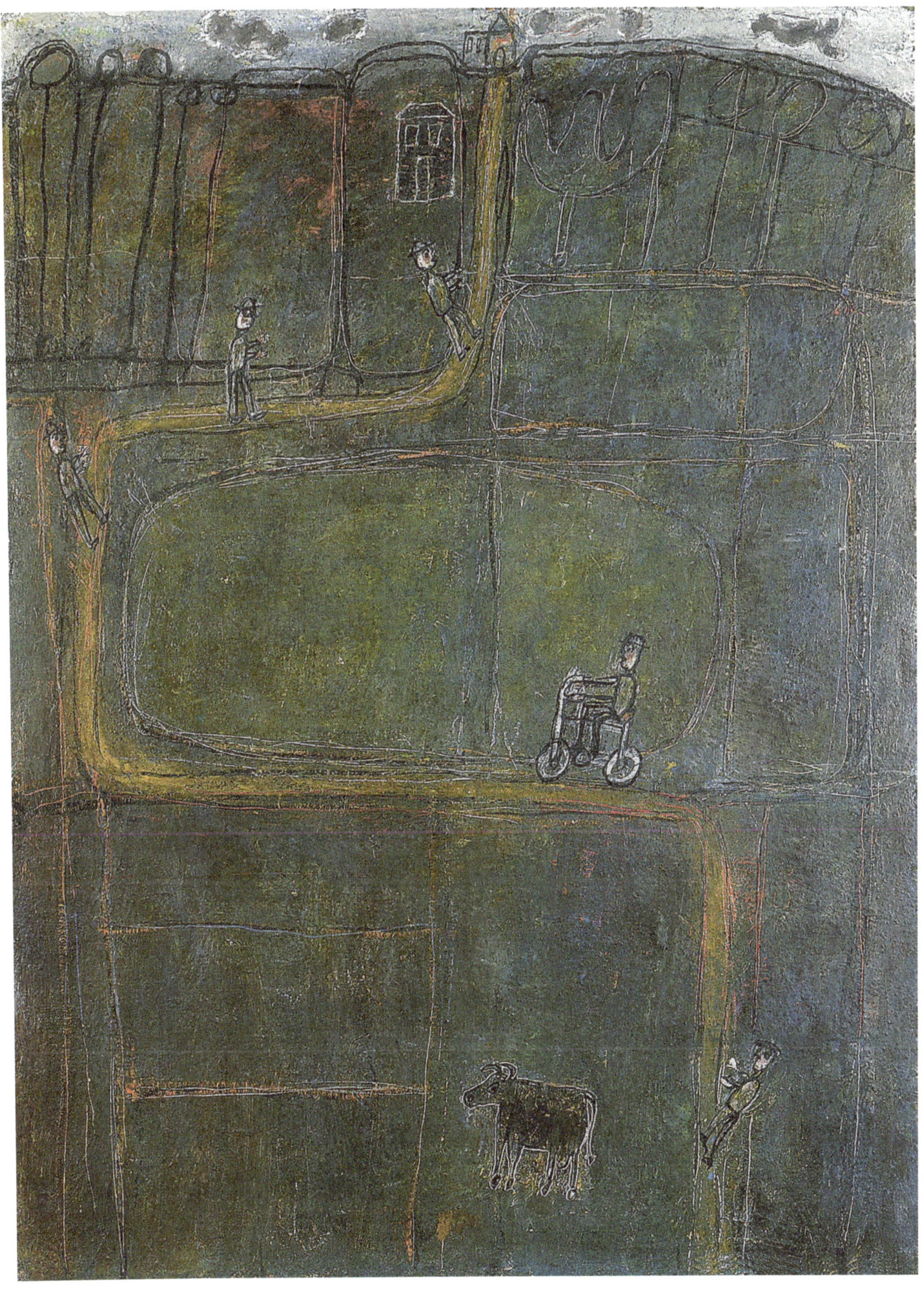

LIST OF ILLUSTRATIONS

ART HISTORY COLLECTION

Abstract Art

Art Deco

Art Nouveau

Baroque

Byzantine Art

Chinese Art

Cubism

Dada

Early Italian Art

Egypt Art

Expressionism

Gothic Art

Greek Art

Impressionism

Indian Art

Naive Art

Neoclassicism

Persian Art

Post-Impressionism

Realism

Renaissance

Pre-Raphaelites

Rococo

Roman Art

Romanesque Art

Romanticism

Surrealism

Symbolism

The Fauves

The Viennese Secession